GW00673739

Dear Reader

It feels like forever since we last held a Pictoplasma publication in our hands, fresh from the printer. 2020 has been such a challenge, with most social interaction forced into the digital realm, so it seems like a miracle to return to the haptic and tactile delight of printed matter.

Back in 2019, when planning for our then upcoming Berlin festival, we decided to dedicate a special focus on the mask in contemporary visual culture, developing an extended performance programme and symposium that explored masks in art, fashion, protest and robotics. We never could have envisioned that a global pandemic would soon make masks an essential accessory in our everyday reality.

As the focus of our research evolved with the crisis, we were grateful for the works and words of a broad range of contributing artists, academics, activists and curators who we present here, many of whom were part of our first digital conference, *Pictoplasma 2020 – in Isolation*, which attracted nearly 100k views around the globe and remains available on pictoplasma.com/pictotalks.

Beyond the mask, this magazine also offers a peak at current trends in the world of character design, featuring work by leading international artists and upcoming talent discovered through our community network pictofolio.com. The magazine is faithfully numbered #1. We hope for the physical delight of many more issues in the future.

Yours sincerely   Peter & Lars

Contents

Nadine Redlich
lives and works as
a cartoonist in
Düsseldorf. She is
a renowned edito-
rial illustrator
whose work includes
a weekly column in
Zeit Magazin. Nadine
published the ten-
sion-easing *Ambient
Comics*, the stress
opus *Paniktotem*,
and her hateful love
letter *I Hate You –
You Just Don't Know
It Yet* with Rotopol.

nadineredlich.de

Nadine Redlich

Twee Muizen

Melancholic Masks

When we make masks, we find it very attractive to mix surreal
characters with real people. Some masks combine animal
features and mythological or naturalistic elements – others
are normal human faces with really big ears or strange noses.
Applying embroidery technique to the masks allows us
to design the face and use the colours that we really want.

Cara Mota

Cara Mota

Twee Muizen is the
artistic duo of fine
artist Denis Galocha
and fashion designer
Cris Barrientos, who
grew up in villages
near Santiago de
Compostela, Galicia,
surrounded by moun-
tains, animals and
nature — all of which
plays a dominant
role in their work.

tweemuizen.com

Masks That Work for Themselves

Totsee (2020)

Damselfrau

Pictoplasma: I would like to jump right into your work and talk about the names you give your masks. Do you remember why these names came up and if they mean anything? For example, *Totsee* (2020).

Magnhild Kennedy: That's just short for 'to the sea'. It's because there are nautical elements in the mask. There's coral and brass ornaments that are in the shape of different sea creatures and plants.

P   So, these names float into your head in the process of making, in response to certain materials?

M   No, they show up at the end. I don't think about anything whilst I work. At the end, I look at it and something clear always pops up, then I just fish into that. Say it looks like an owl; what's the Latin word for an owl? I will find the Latin word for an owl. Then change letters so it's not too literal. Maybe it needs more vocals in it, or is it an 'over-toney' mask or an 'under-toney' mask? Does it need some kind of high-note to it? So I put the double 'ee' in the title. It all depends. It's just a question of taste; the exercise of naming them. I try to stay away from literal stuff but sometimes it's just too clear and you can't look away from it.

P   Do the names help to give each mask a certain identity or do you not think in terms of identity?

M   I don't really. Not for me! Because I make a lot, and they're here in boxes laid on top of each other. What are they to me? I think of them like scales that I grow and shed, something like that. I don't look at them as persons or identities. That happens when other people use them. They're not even really masks for me until someone else puts them into action or projects onto them. I will take that on, of course, when I have the experience of someone else having an experience. Then that will imprint on that piece and remain in there.

P   What are they to you before they turn into masks through the action of people wearing them?

M   Just residue. I got into this because of materials. I like the textile experience, the meditative experience. I like texture and colours. For me, it's just about organizing materials. Obviously it is a mask, but I've never had a big interest in masks as the principal category. Therefore, it's rather a question of luck that a mask comes out. Quite often

I really like the ghosts of stuff.

Magnhild Kennedy is a mask maker from Norway, living and working in London. She works under the acronym Damselfrau. The Norwegian word 'damsel' means unmarried woman and the German 'Frau' means woman, historically implying being married. She combines the two words to mean 'married to oneself'. She has collaborated with many artists from the realm of fashion, editorial, art, music and performance.

damselfrau.com

I don't look at them as persons or identities.

I'm surprised that it's functional because I let myself be directed by whatever the material is telling me, and that isn't always functional.

P   There's no drawings, no concept, no sketch?

M   No, I collect a lot of stuff and have lots of boxes with the stuff that I try to organize. Then I just put my hands in there, feel for what feels good, taste-wise and look-wise. It's a different process when I work for someone under commission. Then there's projection from the beginning. This is a whole different process. I often find it quite troublesome because it's not as playful as when I just fiddle around for myself. But that pressure also comes with interesting outcomes that I really like. It's just two very different processes. Both are enjoyable at the end.

P   Those processes where you just play with the material... some of the material has had a meaning before; you took it from somewhere or it has a history. How important is that for you? Do you sometimes have an object that feels so fascinating, you have to do something with it?

M   Absolutely. In the beginning, I started with stuff that had previously functioned as something. I still really like taking apart old clothes and things. My friends bring me things from their travels or something they had in their family. Firstly, it comes with wear, and that's already personality. I can just surf on that, ride on that, and use that information to go faster with what I'm doing. I've always been into stuff that's old because I really like the ghosts of stuff. I don't mean in a mumbo-jumbo way, but I like the feeling of something having been somewhere. That will absolutely inform what I'm doing, will help show me the direction of where the piece is heading. There's often a ghost of the original thing in the mask, it'll have a wink to what it used to be. That will just happen naturally. I don't do it consciously. I try to think as little as possible when I do this.

The masks work for themselves. I can trust their work.

P   There's a profound difference between the face and the mask. Some people say there's no real face and the mask is not a betrayal but just another face. Do you think about these things? And where does the magic happen for you in terms of the relationship between face and mask?

M   It happens when another person wears the mask. I take a picture of it on myself once it's finished and that pretty much rounds up the process of making it. That also provides a conduit to the Internet; I post the image on my different platforms. After that, I never put them on again. That would feel almost incestuous. So, I say; 'Oh, I'm done with that'. But when other people put them into effect, if someone else wears it or photographs it, that's when it becomes a mask. It's their projection that tells me what I'm doing. I'm not that obsessed with the object as a mask until someone else does that for me.

P   And in that moment, what happens? What kind of transformation process is that?

M   I don't know if I can put it into words. It's not a fundamental experience. I'm on the surface all the time. I never really dive down. I'm not a patient person. I have a tendency to leave projects unfinished, and I don't know how this project has managed to continue for eleven years! I think that's just because I let it be, just keep it light. I'm not letting it demand anything from me. I am just so grateful that it turned into work because other people make it into work for me. I'm just playing in this project. It's important for me to keep it super light, very crisp, very playful and not think too much.

P   Another question on that process: You make it, it becomes a mask, you take a photo. In the first phase, it's all about touching and the materiality, as you don't make sketches first. It's playing with the material. But when we perceive it, what's important to the outside world are the images. That's where it happens. But for you, the important thing is the material.

M   I like the image part of it too. I didn't know that it could be like that; the work lending itself so easily to making images. My biggest form of communication happens online. My smartphone is my third arm, I'm on it all the time. The image stuff has become the form of communication. That's where they become real identities, which again has nothing to do with me; that happens out there. They work for themselves. I can trust their work because they do good work for themselves. It is obviously removed from the really tactile place of origin. This later stage is a very different universe and very removed from the original piece. I like both. I like the multidimensionality, that there are so many sides to it where the masks communicate differently. Of course, the important thing is the stuff in the real world. I do shows once in a while, which me and my husband produce ourselves, just to be able to see that the masks can also meet with people in the flesh and do the same kind of job they do on the Internet. But the Internet is super important for me.

P   Let's get back to a time when the Internet wasn't what it is today. Let's go back to the year 2007, around the time that you arrived in London and started going clubbing. Can you tell us how that fed into what you're doing now?

M   We moved from Oslo, and I'm from Trondheim – which is even smaller – to land in London! At that time there was a lot of fashion clubbing, there was this really pumping scene. There was a club called Boombox that was just outrageous; fashion stuff I'd never seen before! People making costumes out of egg cartons and tape, and making it into high-fashion couture. This stuff was so informative for me. I went from zero to a hundred in the way that I took in information and got inspired.

At the same time, my first job was at a vintage designer store called Pallet London in Islington. It stocked lots of couture stuff from the 1940s, 50s and 60s. My boss was very nice to me. He let me sit and do my little stitching stuff behind the till whilst I was looking at all these beautiful old clothes. Some of them were falling apart, and I'd mend them, often learning as I went along. I'd never learned anything technical in terms of working with textiles before.

It's important for me to keep it super light, very crisp, very playful.

With Katja Mayer for *Radical Beauty Project* (2017)

I went from zero to a hundred in the way that I took in information and got inspired.

Mentrix *Nature* (2020)

This hadn't really interested me. I learned about materials and how to work with them, and that led to my first small projects. I was stitching behind the till and that's where the masks started to show up, maybe just because of space restrictions.

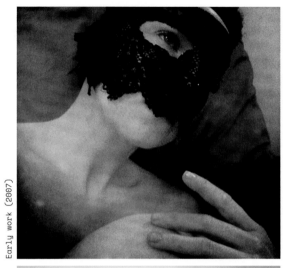

Early work (2007)

Stikker (2012)

In 2012, I cracked the code a little. The few years before had been a bit lacey, a little more sexy; I hadn't found my language, I was just learning technique and finding my footing. I made one piece that was green with some tassels and embroidery. That's probably the most important piece in my whole body of work because when I was making that, I knew that I'd landed. I'd found a space where I could own the work, where I was hoping that it could be work. The shift happened quite early on, and the last eight years have felt quite consistent. I was already at home in the work.

P   Now you're doing a lot of collaborations. Let's take a look at these. You work with artists, fashion editorial, with music people, theatre... how does that happen and what does it do to your masks or your objects?

M   I never search out these collaborations myself. Again, this reflects how I try to keep it really light and easy without trying to determine where the work should go. That's just hoping the work will do that for itself. As I've said before, the Internet is where I communicate. The masks communicate, so they fix their own jobs.

It's always delightful when you see the final product. Then you feel you've communicated, you've

connected to the person wearing it and connected to the project. I love it when the musician Mentrix shows up. She's making a video in Iran in the most beautiful scenery and wants me to make stuff based on traditional headwear there. I find this really difficult because I have very little knowledge of this headwear and culture, so I have to get into that. Seeing that work and being in touch with a culture I know very little of is such a learning curve and makes me have so much more faith in my work. It's such an experience of growth every time, whatever the project.

P   To conclude, let's take a look at a performance group you worked with, the Danish vocal band IKI.

M   This is a cross-Scandinavian vocal group. One of them is Norwegian. She got in touch with me and they flew me over and we did a shoot in Copenhagen. They took good care of me. They're a really cool group of women. On the back of that experience, they commissioned masks for performance. This is a few years ago, and they still wear them and swap them around. Two of them have had babies, so other women will come in and sing when the other two can't, but they wear the same masks. The mask identities are a vehicle for the group. It doesn't matter who's in there. I haven't experienced that before with anyone. Their work is really exceptional and it's always nice to be part of something that I think is really cool.

We have been singing and improvising together for the last ten years. Three years ago, we started collaborating with mask designer Damselfrau. The masks help create space and freedom for us to serve or 'deliver' our music and art, rather than settling into a predetermined 'singer's' role. We create a unit by respecting our differences, and diversity in general, while delivering a unified musical expression.

The award-winning, experimental vocal band IKI consists of five vocalists from Denmark, Norway and Finland. IKI is an ongoing exploration of the human voice with its many facets and sounds. Their approach to their music is improvised, and each concert becomes a unique experience for the audience.

ikivocal.com

Eyewear with a Reason

I am known for making glasses, called *C-Stunners*; '*Cyrus Stunners*'. But they are not masks, neither glasses, they are just simple eyewear. When I start on a new *Cyrus Stunner*, I walk around my area and collect trash. Then I start putting it together. Most of the time I work with pliers, scissors, nails, a hammer. I don't need electricity. I use the original colours from the trash.

I can't start working without having an idea first. If I created without an idea, I would make millions of glasses without any reason. When I make the eyewear, I make them with a reason.

I want to take care of nature through what I am doing. If you are a musician, try to work with nature. If you are a fisherman, please make sure the ocean, the river, the lake is clean. You are in charge of that part. I am in my studio. I am in charge of whatever surrounds me. So, as an artist, my part is to work with trash.

I believe in giving trash a second chance.

Cyrus Kabiru is an artist from Kenya. In addition to wearable facial objects, his sculptural assemblages include abstract bicycles and radios. Cyrus has exhibited on the African continent, in Europe and the USA.

instagram.com/ckabiru

Cyrus Kabiru

Are the Masks That We Wear Against COVID-19 Really 'Masks'?

Christos Lynteris

Christos Lynteris is a medical anthropologist and works as a Senior Lecturer at the University of St Andrews, Scotland. His research focuses on the anthropological and historical examination of epidemics, zoonosis, epidemiological epistemology, medical visual culture, colonial medicine, and epidemics as events posing an existential risk to humanity. He recently completed the project 'Visual Representations of the Third Plague Pandemic', for which he collected and analyzed photographs and other visual documents of the third plague pandemic (1855–1959). The project's OA digital database is available via https://www.repository.cam.ac.uk/handle/1810/275905 Christos has just started a 5-year project on the history of the global war against rats. Given that the pandemic demands social isolation, spending a couple of years in the archives is probably an ideal activity.

Pictoplasma: Could you have expected that the mask, which everybody around the world now wears as a result of the pandemic, would become so ubiquitous?

Christos: Back in February, I expected that if the virus spread across the globe, then the mask would have to be adopted. What I wasn't expecting, perhaps naively, is how difficult this would become and how different people would refuse to wear masks, would doubt the efficiency of the measure or would even construct entire conspiracy theories around it.

P I find it remarkable that people began to understand that masks are predominantly worn to stop the spread of disease and protect others. There was a shift in perspective in regards to the possibility that anyone could have Coronavirus without knowing it, and that's why it is good to wear a mask; to prevent yourself from spreading it. Do you think this was a learning curve for people?

C I think this is still a learning curve. It's very difficult for a lot of people to really become conscious of the fact that they can be spreading the virus without being symptomatic. This is a bit surprising, because there are other diseases that are similar. The parallel I would always draw on is AIDS/HIV. Everyone should be wearing condoms precisely because you may have HIV without having AIDS for the moment. You may be unaware that you have this virus; it's the same thing. But we don't really see a big movement of people burning condoms on the streets like we do with people burning masks. I think it has something to do with the face, the value or the meaning of the face, especially in Western countries.

P Let's go back one hundred and nine years to China, when there was a plague epidemic in 1911. As your research has shown, a type of face mask was developed and used during this time.

C The 1910–1911 outbreak of plague in Manchuria, which was the name used at the time for the north eastern province of China, was part of the so-called third plague pandemic that began in Hong Kong in 1894. It was quite a significant pandemic. It spread across the globe, reached most countries in the world and killed twelve million people. It was within this event that the Manchurian outbreak hap-

We don't really see a big movement of people burning condoms on the streets like we do with people burning masks.

pened. Now, what differentiated the Manchurian outbreak of 1910–1911 was that this was a pneumonic plague outbreak. Normally, plague – the same bacterium – infects the human body creating a pathology that manifests itself in the lymphatic nodes, and that's why we call it the bubonic plague, with these swellings under the armpits or in the groin or the neck. But the same bacterium can cause pneumonic plague, which is when the bacterium infects the lungs. And in this case, plague is contagious. It doesn't require fleas for its transmission but is transmitted through coughing and sneezing. It can kill you within 24 hours from the first symptoms. And the case fatality rate is nearly 100 percent.

Manchuria was controlled by three empires: Japan, Russia and China. The Chinese state had resisted Western medicine, especially the court of the Qing empire. But somehow, they decided to appoint a relatively young guy – Doctor Wu Liande (Wu Lien Teh, 伍連德), who was born in British Penang and educated at the University of Cambridge – as leader of the anti-plague operations. He soon concluded that this was pneumonic plague, and he had a theory that no one else had really developed before; that the disease was transmissible from coughing and sneezing. Therefore, he devised a mask made of gauze and cotton. It was modelled on the surgical mask, which had already existed for about thirteen years, but he adapted this mask into something that could be mass produced because they needed hundreds and thousands of masks on the ground.

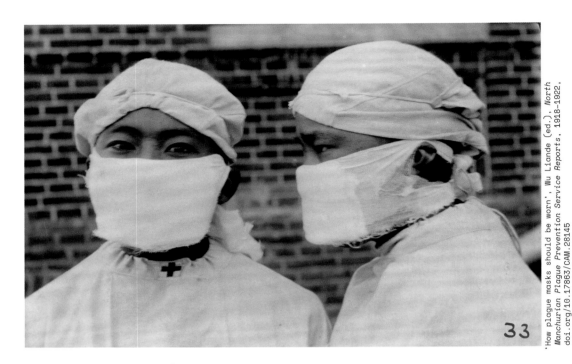

'How plague masks should be worn', Wu Liande (ed.), North Manchurian Plague Prevention Service Reports, 1918–1922. doi.org/10.17863/CAM.28145

And he used the media at his disposal at the time to promote it, which was really, really successful. Newspapers could carry black and white photographs, so within a few weeks or months the entire press across the globe were carrying images of people wearing these masks by Wu Liande, the mask that Wu Liande is himself wearing in this image.

P   Would you say these face coverings not only serve as a means of reducing the spread of the virus but that they also play a role in creating a community, a new and more enlightened society?

C   Yes, I think that's the case with Covid right now; that the mask creates two communities, two at the very least. One community of wearers and another community of non-wearers. It doesn't mean that there is homogeneity within these communities, rather that they can gather around that object on the basis of whether they accept it or deny it.

P   Wu Liande understood that talking about the mask, showing it to people and creating a visual regime, was integral to winning the war against the disease and establishing its general usage. It was also part of China's process into modernity, the political making of China. I know that your research into this is very deep and

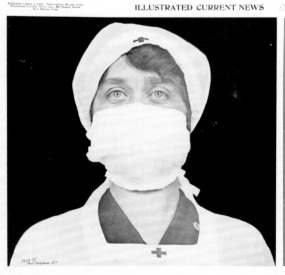

'To prevent influenza', Illustrated Current News, 1918, New Haven, Connecticut, photographer Paul Thompson. resource.nlm.nih.gov/101580385

The mask creates two communities – one community of wearers and another community of non-wearers.

expansive but perhaps you can show us a glimpse of its overriding concerns?

C   One of the big questions, a question that also applies to the masks we wear for Covid, is: are these face covering devices really masks? I'm an anthropologist, and anthropologists have been working on masks for a very, very long time. Not surgical masks or medical masks, but masks used in ritual. One of the main points of agreement is that the mask is not simply a device which covers one's face. More fundamental is that it is a device or an apparatus that transforms the self, the person wearing the mask. Therefore, my question is: did the mask transform the people wearing it, or was it simply a face covering device meant to protect them from viruses? The conclusion I reach from my research is that indeed, it was meant to be a transformative

device. It was meant to be a device which transformed what Dr. Wu saw as a basically non-scientific, or pre-modern kind of population. He had been educated in Cambridge, which meant that he carried a co-lonialist ideology. A reaction to one incident in particular illustrates this: he was very upset when he found out that some people in a town in Shandong province in Chefoo were using the mask only after they had stamped it with a temple seal, transforming it into an amulet, into a magical object.

P   The mask then went into the Western world. How strongly was it used during the global epidemic of Spanish Flu, less than 10 years later?

C   We need more research to actually establish that. There are local studies of use. San Francisco is possibly the most studied case where it became official policy for everyone to wear masks. In other areas it was more voluntary. One of the good things about this current epidemic is that it has created more interest in the history of pandemics and the history of masks. As such, we're going to see a lot of work coming from historians about the flu pandemic of 1918–1919 and the use of masks across different contexts.

In early April 2020, Pictoplasma's community site Pictofolio invited international creatives to join the #FaceValue call for entries. The requirements were: stay home, help slow the spread and DIY your very own wearable character mask. The challenge successfully kept artists from all corners of the globe indoors for a while, helped add some valuable character to the bore-out of self-isolation, and once the first wave's curve had temporarily flattened enough to allow the world to get a little livelier, encouraged artists to show off their awesome creations, often scaring people into keeping their required social distance!

pictofolio.com

FaceValue

Ryan Quincy
Los Angeles, United States
@ryan_quincy

Adéle Cload
Bath, United Kingdom
@adele_cload

Aniko Takacs
Hungary
@anikotakacs

Harmonie Aupetit
Nanterre, France
@harmonieaupetit

Tasha Levytska
Kiev, Ukraine
@tasha_levytska

James Lassey
Vertou, France
@doudoupop

Tanda
San Francisco, United States
@tanda

Mateo Romero
Mexico City, Mexico
@mateo_romero

Rafa Mlon
Mexico City, Mexico
@mlon

Dante
Rio De Janeiro, Brazil
@dante

Ben Needham
London, United Kingdom
@ben_needham

Thanee Andino
Bergen, Norway
@thaneerenee

Larissa Honsek
Berlin, Germany
@larissahonsek

Sjors Houkes
Berlin, Germany
@sjorshoukes

Farah Noor
Croatia
@farah_noor

Jhonatan Correa (Ziggy)
Rionegro, Colombia
@cyberzig

Venetta
California, United States
@venetta

Checomon
Guatemala City, Guatemala
@checomon

Lea Kirdikian
Montreal, Canada
@junkmunkez

Ninna Thorarinsdottir
photography by Sigga Ella
Reykjavik, Iceland
@ninna

Yas Islas
photography by Ro.belugo
Mexico City, Mexico
@yasmini

As a creature performer, I work with costumes that swallow me up completely. This is one of the greatest challenges in my practice but it is also what I love the most about it. There is a real sense of freedom when my face is not visible, but then I have the challenge of communicating everything about the character through the costume. I have to extend the performance of a normal actor who works with their real body into a body that is outside and larger than myself and often doesn't look like me. That is really exciting. As humans, we are used to moving about, making gestures with our faces and hands, and we basically know how other people will respond to that. When I smile, people will think I am happy. But if I make the same gestures in the suit, it's not gonna happen. Therefore, I need to find an entirely new vocabulary. I have to look at the shape of the creature, of the costume I am in and consider how my movements can convey the emotions that the character is feeling. I try to create that internally and map it onto a different physicality. I need to find out how to make this creature move so it looks alive and has the full emotional spectrum that we would expect from any character. In general, when working in these big suits, the gestures have to be bigger. I am taking this larger-than-life feeling into the suit.

Jeremiah Krage is an actor specialising in bringing non-human creatures to life, including iconic television roles such as Tinky Winky in the *Teletubbies* and the Cyberman in *Doctor Who*. His interest in playful creativity extends beyond performance to encompass installations and interactive public art.

thepracticalcreative.life

Jeremiah Krage

Guillaumit

Augmenting Carnival

Guillaumit is an illustrator, graphic and motion designer from Bordeaux. His work combines geometric forms, rigid colour schemes and a funny cartoon style to build a universe of characters that is both playful and serious.

guillaumit.tumblr.com

In 2018, I was appointed artistic director for the carnival in Bordeaux. My first question was; how can we make an interesting carnival today, in the age of social media, face-tracking and mobile phones? With this in mind, I decided to make an augmented reality carnival. At every public event, we are confronted with an incredible number of phones. I decided to work with this relation and use the phone as a basis of interaction between the public and the performers. We developed an augmented reality app and made masks, posters, and costumes with augmented reality for the carnival. In 2020, we focused on the climate crisis and rising sea level as a theme for the carnival's edition. We imagined a future where we all live under water, and created mutant character costumes.

threadstories

When Did Exposure Become a Currency That We Trade In?

Irish visual artist threadstories' work is an interplay between craft, performance, photography, film and social media. She is questioning how the erosion of personal privacy in our digital age affects how we view and portray ourselves online. Her malleable textile masks are feverishly preened, animated and reworked, the same mask reinventing itself continually.

instagram.com/threadstories

Pictoplasma: The first question that I feel I need to ask is about the images on your Instagram and beyond. Do you want to reveal who the model is? Is it always the same person? Is it relevant for you to reveal their identity?

threadstories: It's a one woman show. I make, I perform, I capture. It's all me. It is relevant that it's a selfie because I'm kind of 'poking' at social media. The fact that I have these manufactured facades and I'm showing them through the platforms of social media... the selfie aspect is important.

P We will come to the selfie and social media later, but let's take a look at what we see in your work. We can often see through the masks to the face behind. The faces aren't completely covered. There is a translucency or transparency to your masks. What does that mean for you?

t It's fun to play with features, and what you can see and can't see.

I'm disrupting how you see the person underneath. You can't really figure out all the visual cues we usually rely on, such as seeing how attractive someone is, seeing how youthful someone is, maybe being able to gaze their emotion. I am disrupting all of this with the mask, so sometimes you see a bit more of me in some images than others. It's all playing, playing with how you can make a judgement about me.

P How about eye contact? The mask can have eye contact, but the person underneath can also have eye contact, thanks to the translucency of the mask. You can have both at once. Do you play with that?

t When I make masks that have no obvious face, I can see it leaves the viewer quite cold. People need to see the face in the mask. They need to feel that there is someone underneath that mask. When the mask is left completely blank, there is a real disconnect. I find that when I make

Untitled (2019)

eye contact with the viewer, there is a bigger response.

P   Let's switch to the process of making them. Do you have a routine to get inspired? How you approach a piece of work?

t   It's all about materials. Everything starts with the material. I will move through the studio; I have collected and gathered a lot of materials over the years everything from regular wool and yarns to rope and thread and ribbons. I'll have a touch, I'll have a feel. I start to put things side by side. I'll think, 'Uh, I haven't tried that before'. If I can see the mask in my head before I make it, I sense that I shouldn't make it, because it's not going to surprise me. I always like to start with the materials and see what starts to unfold.

Everything is crochet, that's my technique for building. Then I often hand-tuft, which is how I add the sense of volume. I'm always using the same two techniques, but then I try to be as experimental as I can within that limitation. I don't really use reference material, I consider everything to be reference material, from people's teeth that I see when I go shopping, to fine art, to absolutely everything.

P   Everything you do is self-initiated. Do you sometimes work with other people? Are there any commissions or requests for certain masks? And if so, how do you respond?

t   In the beginning, it was definitely all me. Now, I get a lot of requests for commissions. I don't take on many commissions, because I don't consider myself to be a designer. I like to make what I want to make. I definitely consider myself to be more of a visual artist who doesn't work to a brief. It depends on who comes my way, if I am interested or not.

P   I will read out three keywords, and you can tell me if they resonate. The first is 'grotesque'.

t   I would hope so, at times.

P   The other one would be 'fetish'.

t   Not for me, but I can see other people responding to my work like that.

P   The third one is 'gender'.

t   It's interesting to disrupt people's assumptions about who is underneath. I think my eyes possibly suggest that I am a female. The masks are manufactured facades. They are supposed to be a mix between the real and the unreal, the known and the unknown. They are a middle-ground between lots of things.

P   Let's talk about the relationship between face and mask. There is a paradox. The face is authentic, as it expresses our feelings. We can read the feelings of others in their faces. Then the mask covers that up, hides that. How do you think through this relationship between the authentic face and the betraying mask?

t   I am always quite interested in some of the phrases that we use, for instance, when women put on makeup, they 'put on their face'. I am interested in how we interact with our faces, and how the digital age, over the last twenty years, has completely blown up our relationship to our faces in

I consider everything to be reference material.

I'm disrupting how you see the person underneath.

terms of how we can edit our images. We can sanitise images of our faces and we can manipulate our own face. This is a very recent phenomenon. That really interests me. I am always interested in how people are reshaping their faces, whether virtually or in real life. I don't know if that answers your question?

P   It does, but let's put it another way. The face is directed towards other people. You say that in the past twenty years, that game has changed completely because 'the other person'

is becoming anonymous. I don't know who is seeing or watching me, whether it's via social media or in the public space, through CCTV. So, the ethics of the face, this connection to the other person, is really upside down. How does your work fit into this as a statement?

t   I consider privacy to be precious. I think it's interesting that we give away our faces because they have now become something through which people can earn money. I am quite interested in surveillance capitalism, how our faces in the public domain are used in ways we don't yet understand. It's already happening that you can walk into a shopping centre and they can pick up who you are from social media images and target you with specific items. They can get an idea of your age range and what you might be interested in from what you've been exploring online. That's already happening. I feel that privacy is very precious and we shouldn't necessarily give it away.

I use the term *anti-celeb*, and I think that came about because people used to contact me and say, 'We would like to use your masks and it will be great exposure'. I started to think, when did exposure and everybody knowing your face and who you are become a currency that we trade in? When did being known become coveted? And why is there this assumption that we all want to be known, or we all want our five minutes of fame? That terminology

Falsehood series (2019)

I use – *anti-celeb* – is about rejecting that, rejecting the bedroom celebrity. But I guess I am a bedroom celebrity of sorts, so what can I say?

P   I guess that in the second half of the 20th century, it was TV. Andy Warhol said that everyone would get their five minutes of fame on TV. Now that game has changed, now everyone can achieve this through social media. That's where you attack. I think thread-stories is like an anti-movement on the core platforms. You don't wear a mask locally when you go shopping to avoid CCTV, but you wear it on the platform that trades in the currency of the face.

t   One hundred percent. That's why I think threadstories fits very naturally and comfortably on that platform. It's equivalent to self-publishing, you can bypass the gatekeepers in the art world and go straight to your audience on social media. It's an interesting platform to explore ideas, if you're not just using it to show your friends what you are up to.

P   This year's Pictoplasma has a special focus on the mask.

Coincidentally, everybody is wearing a mask because of the pandemic. Do you think that the current phenomenon of everybody wearing a mask will have an effect on your work? And in the long-run, how do you think this will effect society in terms of privacy?

t   I am a mask maker, but I never thought I would see the day that I would be doing my grocery shopping in a mask. It will take a few years for me to percolate and make a judgement on what I think is happening at the moment. I enjoy listening to the debate, and I suppose that different countries have different debates around the resistance to mask wear-ing. I enjoy thinking about where this comes from or what this means. I also think it's interesting how quickly people adapt, and how something that would have seemed absolutely extraordinary in January has now become commonplace.

I think a mask for personal protection is different to a mask for disguise. I find it interesting that, at least here in Ireland, it's been reported that there was a delay with men wearing masks, as if protecting themselves made them less macho or something. There are all these kernels of information that are probably going into my head and will manifest at some stage in the work I make.

Why is there this assumption that we all want to be known?

Untitled (2020)

Falsehoods (2018), photo by Hazel Coonagh

A mask for personal protection is different to a mask for disguise.

The Future of 3D Makeup

Ines alpha is a 3D artist based in Paris who worked as an art director in advertising with a focus on beauty and luxury. After her first steps into AR with an experimental music video, she developed a passion for virtual makeup. Ines is finding ways to imagine total aesthetic freedom for one's appearance and encourages a fun and creative approach to self-expression with a clear message: We need to de-dramatize beauty!

inesalpha.com

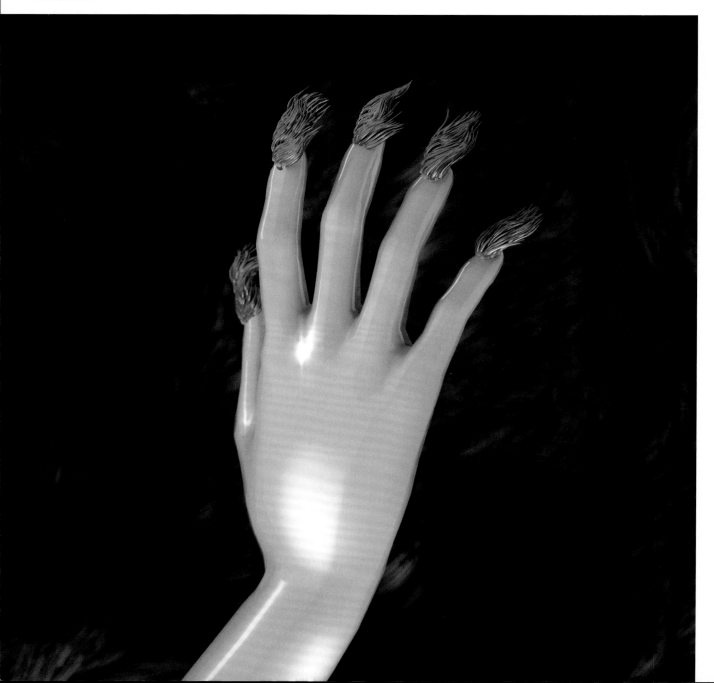

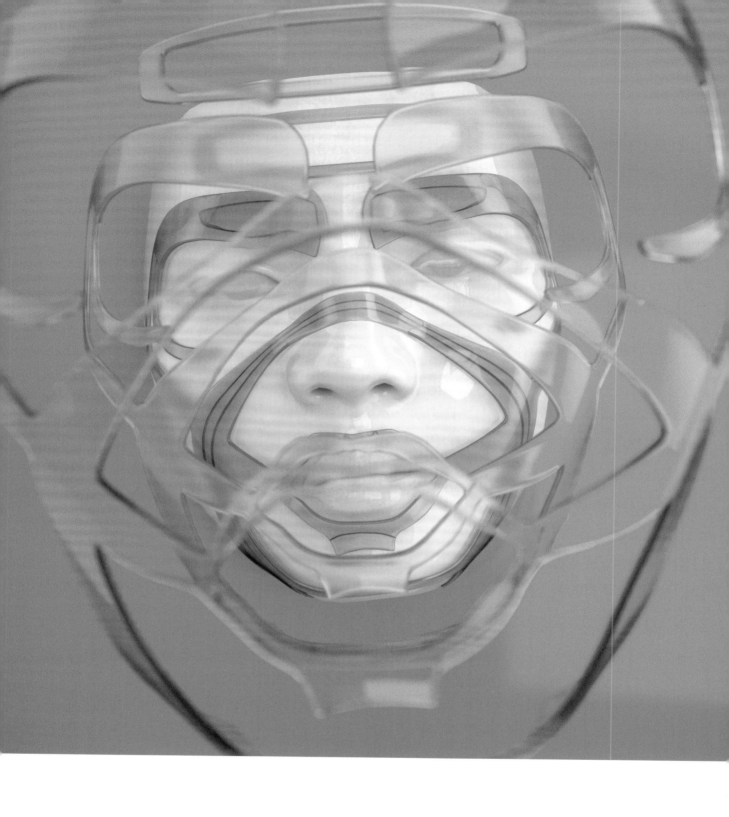

Pictoplasma: What is 3D makeup?

Ines alpha: For me, makeup is self-transformation. Makeup is transforming someone's face with any tool you can get. Until now, it's been eyeshadows, mascara, powders, pigments, but lately people have been transforming with other tools, with objects, props, with plastic surgery. So, why not transform yourself with digital software?

Why 3D makeup?

I was fascinated by this huge trend I noticed amongst artists, makeup artists and performers who were transforming themselves in new ways that I hadn't seen before on the streets, in magazines. I wanted to be part of this new culture. What I like most about 3D software is that I can imagine things that are not doable in the physical world. With 3D tools I can create my own reality. I can defy gravity and create shapes and textures that don't yet exist in the physical world.

How can you make your art accessible to everyone? How can 3D makeup be the future of makeup?

We are already wearing it, using augmented reality. An AR filter is a computer-generated effect that you can add on  yourself in real time using your smartphone. There are filters you can use on both Instagram and Snapchat, who have both launched their own augmented reality software. I thought this could be the way for me to democratise my work and make this new kind of makeup accessible to everyone.

What parameters do you set yourself when designing your filters and 3D makeup, in order to go beyond mere decorating and be able to transform a face into something really different?

There are zones on the face that I like to work with and know intuitively, maybe because I've worked in makeup so much. I know that when you highlight the cheek, when you put something on top of the cheek, it looks good. I know that if you add something to the chin, it can look bad because it looks like a beard. Our eyes are educated to think something looks bad. The first time I did a design that went all around the face – because I was imagining some kind of flower – I thought; it looks weird. Some people think that my work is really creepy, not beautiful, and I totally understand that. I want to show that weird can be cool and open people's minds to a different kind of beauty.

I'm wondering about the ways in which people can wear this kind of makeup and where it would make sense to wear it or try it out. For instance, filters only work online or on digital images, but our perception of the here and now is non-digital. Do you think this will change?

At first, I thought about how we can wear virtual makeup in the physical world. I thought that maybe it would be possible with 3D printing and some robotics, but it started to become very complicated to produce. I thought that maybe holograms could be used in the future. Then I saw an article about how contact lenses with built-in nanotechnology are being developed. With those, we'll be able to see everyone through filters – see anything – with our own eyes. It's gonna be very real and it's gonna be very soon because technology develops so fast.

Julian Glander is
a 3D artist based
in the USA. Being
bad at illustration
encouraged him to
create his latest
game *Art Sqool*,
featuring an AI art
teacher who assigns
over 200 inspiring
prompts to players,
helping them break
through any creative
block.

glander.co

The Uncharted Territories of Face Filters

David OReilly is a multidisciplinary artist based in Los Angeles. Starting his career as an independent animator, he created numerous award-winning short films, has written for TV shows such as *Adventure Time* and *South Park* and created the fictional video games in Spike Jonze's movie *Her*. David is the creator of the iconic game *Mountain* and the universe simulation game *Everything*.

davidoreilly.com

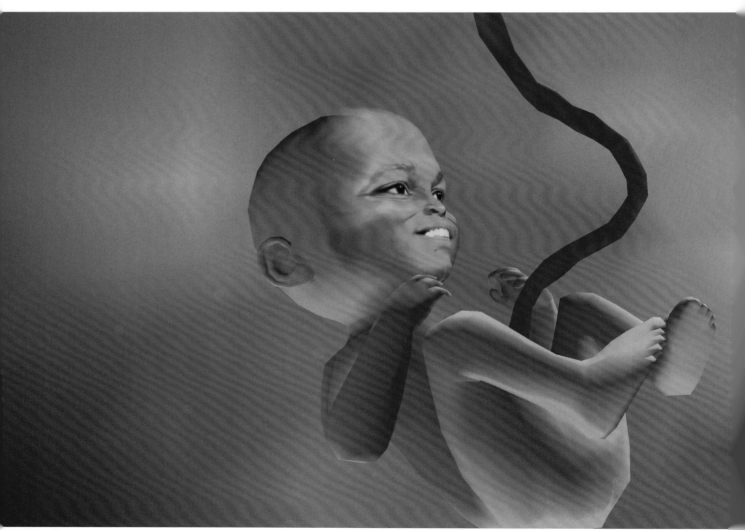

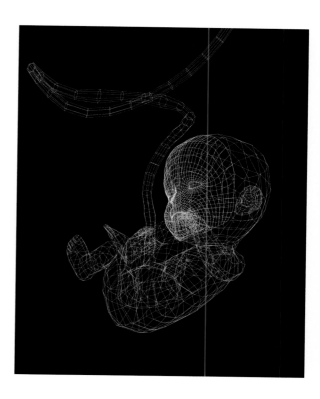

Pictoplasma: You seem to seamlessly shift through genres – first you shook things up in the world of animation film, then we saw you go into games and redefine the media, so to speak, and now you're working with face filters. How much of a challenge is it for you to keep establishing yourself in new areas?

David OReilly: I suppose that from the outside, it does look like I'm jumping from thing to thing. These mediums have different people pushing them, different tools that are used to make them and different people writing about them. But there's a common thread running through it all, which is this evolution of 3D software, or more generally, a form of 3D – you could even say 4D, or even dimensions beyond that.

Essentially, it's still one journey. I am just looking at what's available and trying to adapt and not be too nostalgic for older forms that would hold me back. When I started out with 3D animation, which is now considered a very established form, it had this feeling of being very, very new and if you were jumping into that, then it was almost as though you were leaving 'the real animation' and going off to explore some other new artistic thing.

Another thing connecting the way I work with all of this is the fact that I've almost always used real time rendering, even in the animated works. Almost all of my animation films are rendered in real time, basically from screen capture. That includes the *Adventure Time* episode and U2 video and even commercial things. They were all rendered in a very simple way.

P   Leaving the technical side of things for a moment, I know that your filters have been extremely popular. How is that measured? In downloads or clicks? Can you give us a brief idea of how popular they are?

D   They're measured in views. I wish I knew exactly how many different individuals look at them. I only have the numbers of people who open them in some form or other, whether they open their own version or my version or someone else's post or whatever. But that number is in the billions. Over approximately two billion views. People make around 100,000 videos a day with my effects, which always surprises me! If I make a new one, I'll get millions of views per day. Sometimes there are mini-explosions. For example, right now there's an Indonesian comedian who's built a whole career using a part of one of my effects.

P   Is that nice for you? Is it flattering or does it feel a bit strange?

D   It's brilliant. I absolutely love it. With this kind of work – and maybe this will sound cliched or sentimental or whatever – it's really only completed when other people start filling it up. I'm not a

There's this element to it that you can't control; what people will do with it or how they'll react.

performative sort of person; I don't think I've ever posted myself using these particular effects, but I absolutely love that other people do so.

There's this element to it that you can't control; what people will do with it or how they'll react. That's the nature of all games and interactive stuff. You're only bringing 50 percent and then the people bring the other half. I feel that all art is interactive in this way, and I don't want to say it only happens with interactive stuff, but it's more obvious or clear.

P   Seeing how your face filters reverberate on such a global scale, is it necessary to limit them to one very easy, understandable story so that everyone in the world can understand? A story such as 'birth and death', as in *Simulation* (2019)?

D   It's easy to look at my effects now and say they are clearly designed for mass-consumption or a mass-market. People had been making effects and filters on Instagram for about a year or so before I started making my effects, but nobody had done anything similar to any of these things.

It makes sense to create something that has immediacy because people's minds are conditioned to only sustain an entropy or an interest level for about three seconds when it comes to effects. People aren't used to these effects continuing beyond three seconds.

The *Simulation* effect lasts about two and a half minutes and has this quite elaborate narrative that takes place, using your face as the main character.

P   Usually, face filters are meant to enhance or beautify appearance and identity, the expression of self. But I don't see that at all with your face filters. I see 'David' in these filters because you are hijacking the users to tell a story. You are interested in narration, in a way that face filters usually aren't. That's what makes your face filters so complex; you are not just applying a new form or a new self on someone. You are hijacking their face. You are casting them, if you like, to star in your movie.

D   My first experiments with the effects were all distortions; how to distort someone's face in a way that wasn't necessarily beautiful. The most popular effects on Instagram are decorative, adding makeup, sparkles and things like that. These are by far the most popular. I have absolutely no interest in that, and that comes from a very fundamental place: I don't think anything is more beautiful or compelling or interesting than the reality that enters our eyes. When you start to decorate that, you might as well be putting clown makeup on everything. This kind of decoration is beautiful in its own way, but only in how it reveals the specifics of how we define beauty and the limitations of that. To be honest with you, I have a repulsion to a lot these effects that have a 'plastic surgery' type of result.

I know that Facebook has been trying to clamp down on that. It's one of the few things they're doing that I feel glad about. Obviously, people can do whatever they want, but effects that enable a kind of virtual plastic surgery are very, very difficult to justify. I think that they will warp our image of ourselves.

If you look at the discussion forums for augmented reality effects, most people are complaining that their 'plastic surgery' effect isn't getting them 100,000 followers quickly enough. It's sad. I don't want to impose my morals on anybody, but I don't find this stuff interesting on a creative level. We're dealing with uncharted territory in playing with images of ourselves. Instagram is already doing a lot of damage at a basic level by promoting certain types of beauty. The direction of this whole thing is not very interesting.

P   Do you think that the pandemic times will have any influence on how these filters and this whole culture develops?

D   Of course. Now we appear in digital form more and more. Most interactions that we're having with one another are virtual. We're all used to Zoom and Skype and whatever else. A lot of people that were working in AR and VR were publicly decrying the tragedy of the pandemic and privately celebrating it, because they've been preparing for this dystopian reality for quite a while, and they've got it.

P   They're happy.

D   Yeah, I think they're secretly high-fiving inside their heads. Inside their brain are two virtual hands clapping. And they're saying: Thank God I've devoted my life to a world where humans never have to actually see each other.

They've been preparing for this dystopian reality for quite a while, and they've got it.

P   I have one last question for you. You have made an incredible name for yourself as an independent film-maker and then you became an independent game-maker. Would you now consider yourself an independent face filter maker?

D   Many different people – agents, managers, musicians and companies and so on – have asked me to make more advanced effects for their brands and I've said no to every single one. That is motivated by the fact that it is impossible to be independent with the filters because they are very much tied into formats that exist and are not yet open formats. It's wonderful that I can create a virtual world that operates like the real time world, and people can access it by just tapping something without downloads or drivers, no crap.

The confluence of technologies in a phone, even in an app like Instagram, is stunning. That's why I'm drawn to this. The form in which a filter exists is a bunch of mathematical nodes, just endless webs. In order to develop this in a truly open way... there is no tool to do that yet.

P   As an artist trying to express yourself, you are now completely dependent on, locked in by and tied to Instagram or Facebook, which is the same thing anyway, as Facebook owns Instagram.

D   Yeah, absolutely. I don't create effects for hire partly because most people are not looking for something that's particularly interesting or ground-breaking. But it's also because there is a quiet, unspoken race between what happens in the world of art – I'm not talking about 'the art world', but the world of creativity – and the world of commerce. We've seen it for the last twenty years; somebody creates something interesting in the animation world, independently, then it just gets eaten and torn apart by agencies and brands, other actors, people who are more commercially focused, until you forget all about the original. This has happened to almost every interesting animator since the dawn of time.

But for the last thirty years, let's say, it's been very obvious. Therefore, I think it's very positive that somebody like me, a person just by myself, without a team, can basically create works that are so far ahead of what any agency can do. That's a really rare position to be in. All the interesting things are happening at the level of individuals, and I think that's a great thing.

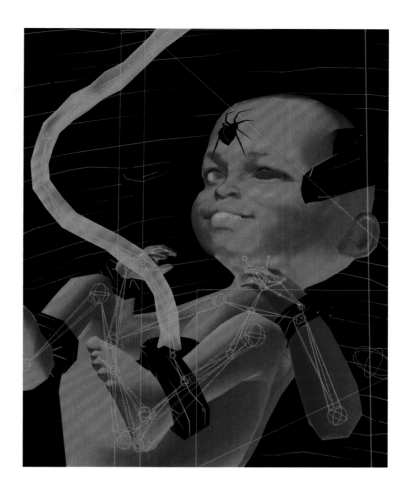

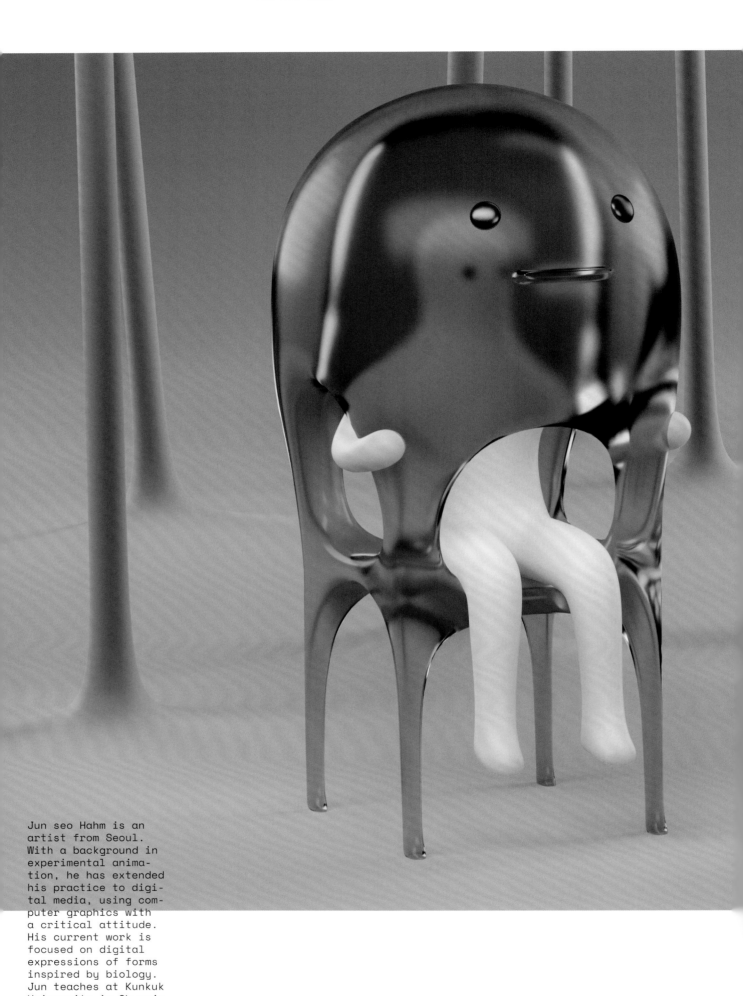

Jun seo Hahm is an
artist from Seoul.
With a background in
experimental anima-
tion, he has extended
his practice to digi-
tal media, using com-
puter graphics with
a critical attitude.
His current work is
focused on digital
expressions of forms
inspired by biology.
Jun teaches at Kunkuk
University in Chungju
and is a PhD candi-
date studying with
a focus on art and
technology in arti-
ficial life at Sogang
University, Seoul.

junseohahm.com

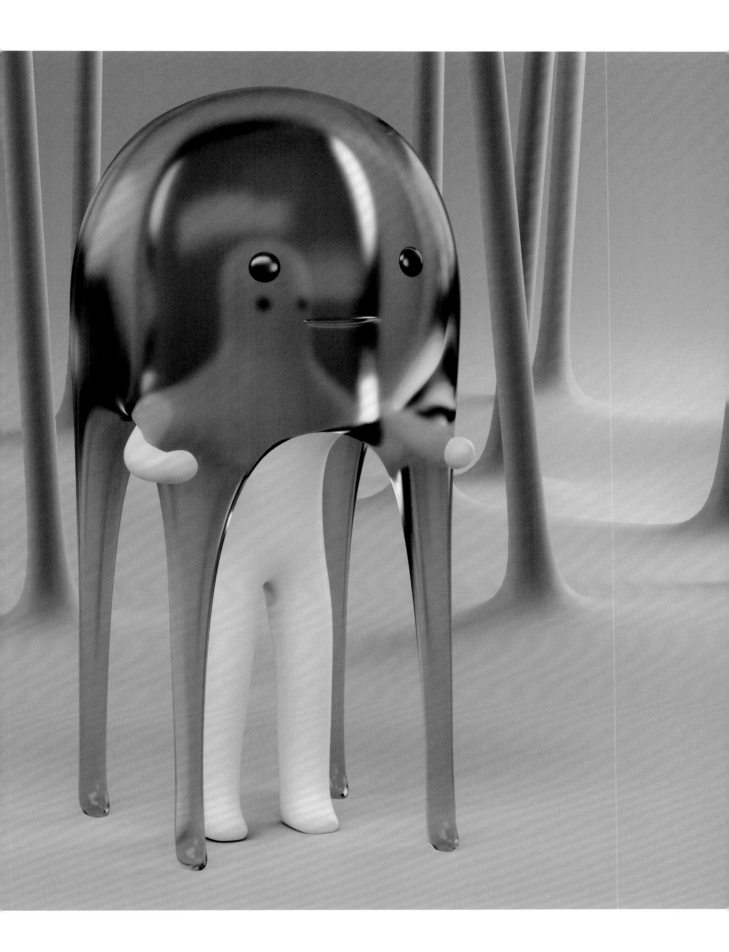

Jun seo Hahm

RNNT

We are a collective involved in artistic creation that combines sound with visual arts. We have been wearing masks on stage since the launch of the project because we care more about physical spectacle than personalities.

BNNT are Konrad Smoleński and Daniel Szwed. They produce audio performances that are variously held in the pub- lic spaces of towns and cities or the institutionalised spaces of galleries and festival venues. Throughout a decade of activity, their endeavours have con- stantly resisted any kind of labelling, covering a wide spec- trum between sight and sound.

bnnt.pl

Collective Kahilo

Capuchas in Chile's Feminist Struggle and Beyond

Capucha – a hoodie, a piece of cloth wrapping your face, a sophisticated sequined cloth mask, or a snowshoe: all ways to cover up your identity and pursue the freedom of anonymity in political protest. In Chile, the *capucha* has played a fundamental role in the feminist struggle and in the protests that have occurred since their outbreak on October 18, 2019. Collective Kabilda is a feminist collective of women living in Berlin united by the Chilean revolution, who, inspired by the mobilizations in Chile, decide to integrate the hood as an honour and connection with the Chilean struggle.

Pictoplasma: First of all, what is a *capucha*?

Maite: It started out as a piece of cloth, like a T-shirt or a kerchief, used to cover the face. At demonstrations, it serves more to protect from tear gas and pepper spray. At the same time, it shields the wearer from political and police persecution. Wearing a mask provides anonymity.

This is nothing new: the Zapatista struggle wore *capuchas* and they're still used today, but more commonly balaclavas, which are symbols of resistance, as the majority of Mexico's native peoples were ignored by the government. By covering their faces, they made their struggle visible, not only in Mexico but to the entire world. A strategy for the people who had no voice.

P   What is the specific way feminist movements make use of the *capucha*?

M   It's quite similar in the context of feminism. Masks are used to denounce the inequalities and violence suffered by women and non-binary individuals around the world under the patriarchal system. Chilean women in particular feel much safer and more comfortable protesting with a *capucha*. It also allows them to represent not only an individual but a collective identity. What makes feminist *capuchas* special is the fact that they're embellished: with

Subcomandante Marcos, the spokesman of the Ejército Zapatista de Liberación Nacional, Chiapas, Mexico 1996, photo by Jose Villa

sequins, pearls, different fabrics, sometimes even plaits. But it's always a symbol of rebellion.

P   Can you give us examples of how the *capuchas* were used in political protest in Chile recently?

Constanza: There are two decisive milestones here. Firstly, in May 2018 the Chilean feminist movement reached a point of no return when women from across the country began making demands. Female university students began to protest against sexist attitudes in the classrooms. The protests escalated across the country, targeting universities that have historically protected the perpetrators rather than their victims. In this context, the perpetrators range from fellow students to professors, all men.

The 'Feminist May' consolidated Chile's new women's rights movement in public opinion: from theory to the street, on social media, in the mass media and even in the political arena. We hadn't seen a women's movement for social causes of this size since the dictatorship. These protests also gave consideration to non-binary women and dissidents, bringing about a cultural and generational shift where empowered women are instigators and leaders of current political and social changes.

In mid-October 2019, the administration of Sebastián Piñera announced a 30-peso fare hike on underground rail transport, the Santiago Metro. Secondary school pupils were the first to react to this increase, and with the slogan 'evade, don't pay, another way to fight', they called for mass fare-dodging tactics with collective actions at different stations throughout the city. Female secondary school students were the ones who jumped turnstiles and began leading protests. They rallied to cries of 'It's not about 30 pesos, it's about 30 years' and 'Chile Woke Up', making it clear that the people demanded a change in public policies related to transport, health, education, pensions, natural resources, reproductive and sexual rights.

On the street, the *capucha* granted protestors a militant collective identity during the uprising, where the people appropriated and reclaimed the public space and a mutual support system, having been abandoned by the state and its institutions. It's important to note that the systematically violent onslaught of the militarised Chilean police didn't just mutilate the eyes of hundreds of protestors. Reviving a practise from the days of the dictatorship, feminised bodies were also subjected to political and sexual violence in the form of harassment, threats and intimidation, abuse and even rape.

photo by Gonzalo Maturana Hurtado

Maite: I think the performance by Las Tesis, *A Rapist in Your Path* – a very moving denunciation of sexual violence against women – marked a historic turning point and was an expression of collective sorority that made itself visible in practically every part of the world. An important accessory in that performance was the blindfold. For me, it represented a visible reminder of how society and state institutions turn a blind eye to violence against women. With that performance, feminists made their voices heard in the Chilean uprising. It was a moment of empowerment for women; they began to get organised, and suddenly we saw lots of groups of women dancing at marches and fighting at protests, and many of them were wearing capuchas.

photo by Gonzalo Maturana Hurtado

And more: a structural change with a new constitution to replace the existing one inherited from Pinochet. The wave of protests grew and spread across the country, and the *capucha* became a habit for protestors. It's also an emblem of the uprising, for reasons which, as Maite explained, have to do with protecting one's identity; furthermore, *capuchas* were absolutely necessary given the toxic gases released by the police, which rendered entire neighbourhoods unbreathable.

I remember watching these events from a distance, from an alternate reality where the protests have not made such a significant difference in everyday life, much less a structural difference. I watched it via screens, in a different season of the year and in another time zone.

"Aquí se titulan violadores"

Estudiante UC

LA UC ENCUBRE EL ABUSO

¿Quieres entrar en la UC?
Abuso garantizado

photo by Rodrigo Henry Gálvez R.

P   You are not living in Chile, but far away in Berlin. What did it mean for you to witness what was going on?

C   I remember watching these events from a distance, from an alternate reality, and from here it seems as though the protests have not made such a significant difference in everyday life, much less a structural difference. I watched it via screens, in a different season of the year and in another time zone. I remember trying to sleep and sometimes waking up from nightmares, confused as to why I'm not running from the police, and even more confused because no one around me felt it and understood it as I did.

M   I knew, we all knew, that the 8th of March, International Women's Day, was approaching, and I felt the need to create something similar to what was happening with the feminist movement in Chile and the uprising. So, I got together with a few other women and we decided to organise a *capucha* workshop here in Berlin. Just as I had imagined, the workshop turned out beautifully. We had between twenty and thirty women, and each brought her own

materials, which we shared. It was a warm, welcoming atmosphere, filled with interesting conversations. We felt that it was a safe space, a place of trust and abundant creativity. At the end, we were all very proud of our *capuchas*, made with love. In a way it was a tribute, an action expressing solidarity with what was happening in Chile, and we felt that we were somehow part of that.

photo by Collective Kabilda

photo by Gonzalo Maturana Hurtado

Craig Green 2012, ATOPOS cvc collection, photo by Yiorgos Mavropoulos

Masks in Fashion is a visual research project by Vassilis Zidianakis, co-founder & artistic director of ATOPOS Contemporary Visual Culture, Athens. ATOPOS cvc is a non-profit cultural organisation interested in the expression and adornment of the human body. The word 'atopos', from the ancient Greek άτοπος, refers to that which is strange, the unwonted, the eccentric and the unclassifiable. It was founded in 2003 by Stamos Fafalios and Vassilis Zidianakis.

atopos.gr #stayhome

Vassilis Zidiniakis

photography Felix Jenkins, instagram.com/jenkins__photography

GodXXX Noirphiles

Occupying a Gender Space in Between

GodXXX Noirphiles (Adrian Marie Blount) is a recent transplant to Berlin from San Diego. Since arriving in Berlin, Adrian has taught anti-racist and collective healing workshops with the F_antifa Kongress, co-created the theatre collective Blackism and is the founder and lead organizer of the drag collective House of Living Colors for exclusively queer and trans BPOC (Black and People of Colour).

instagram.com/godxnoirphiles

Pictoplasma: How did you get started doing drag?

GodXXX Noirphiles: I started doing drag in 2017. It had taken me a while to even give myself permission to do drag, as someone who was assigned female at birth. Even though I identify as non-binary, I still asked myself if I really had a place in drag. I realised that drag is an avenue to explore gender and more specifically, the gender that is placed on you socially. Because I think there is an identified gender; a socially imposed gender that's put onto you, which is also a politically imposed gender. Having given myself the permission to do drag, I asked myself: How am I, as somebody who was assigned female at birth, telling myself that I am not allowed to explore my femininity or not allowed to explore my gender? This was me unpacking my internalised misogyny.

P What does your name 'GodXXX Noirphiles' stand for?

G I wanted to analyse what the world has imposed on me, and this goes into my name. GodXXX is spelled with three XXXs, which is associated with porn and sexualisation, and I use it as an axis to talk about how my body is sexualised, no matter what I wear and no matter which form I am in. Whether I am presenting masculinity, femininity or nothing at all, my body is seen as a sexualised object. And historically, Black femmes have also been sexualised. 'God' speaks to the trope of the 'Magical Negro'. Historically, Black people have been seen as gurus or shamans, a figure who is meant to bring wisdom onto people or help educate. Nowadays, when we talk about critical race theory, people come to Black folks to figure out what they are supposed to do because we are supposed to be those all-knowing beings. And this is where God comes from. My second name, Noirphiles, is 'noir' for black and 'philes' is a derivative from the ancient Greek word for love. So, 'love of Blackness'. A lot of people don't know how to pronounce my name, and I deliberately chose it with that in mind because as a Black body, no matter what name you have, there is always someone who is going to question how to pronounce your name – even if it's really European – simply because you have a Black body. I am reclaiming this in my name, I'm saying I don't care how you pronounce it because it doesn't change the way I feel about my name.

My drag references the *afrofuture*, but also the *afropresent*, because right now what we are living in is the *afrofuture*

photography Tony Stewart
instagram.com/tonystewartphoto

photography Samet Durgun
instagram.com/hi.sametdurgun

to destroy. Activism is a by-product of what we are doing.

P   What is the special function of drag make up? Can you identify the point where a new character is created or born?

G   It's the ritual of adorning myself in makeup and costume that helps me to reclaim my power; a power that I maybe didn't see before. For example, there was a day when I just felt *over it*. I didn't want to do anything, it was overcast... that's when I created this flower look; I needed to bloom and come out of the funk that I was in. I didn't know what I was going to do, but I had these flowers in my house, and they inspired me to create this look. It boosted my energy for the rest of the day, made me feel beautiful. It made me feel seen and colourful, and from the outside in, I was able to transform myself for that day. I think that's what it is; you start with the self, something you interact with every single day and then you perform this ritualistic process of adorning yourself with makeup. Sometimes I don't know what direction 'the look' is going in. When I am building onto my face in relation to my body, I am thinking; what is it that I want to reclaim today? Do I want to reclaim my masculinity? If so, I put on my beard. But when I want to show that I not only love my masculinity but also my femininity, I put on my cut crease eye shadow and lashes, I apply glitter. I am creating this being that is elevated beyond gender. I think that relationship is super important, especially in regards to appreciating my sense of self. When I first got into drag, I was afraid of my masculine side, of exploring that. When people would mis-gender me as 'he', it would make me really angry. My gender is so complex that people have to either impose a gender on me because they are so unsure about what I am, or they have to try and interpret it for themselves. I want to reclaim that for myself.

for my ancestors, who were slaves and never thought it would be possible for me to look like this. This is their idea of futurism, in this moment. I like to reimagine that for myself; what would my future be? My future would allow me to explore gender in any fashion that I chose to explore gender. I would be able to show my body in any facet without it being sexualised. My drag is an amplified me who is from the future, taking hold of their identity and their gender exploration and their being in space and in time.

P   Would you say that drag is a form of activism?

G   There is active activism and there is activism that happens by simply existing in a space. Just being able to perform, any day of the week, as people of colour and exploring this gender in a super non-conforming way; that's activism. When we leave our house, we get heckled on public transport, and then we realise: I just wanted to express my creativity! But this is really political because there is a person over there who is looking at me as if they want to cause me harm, or as if I am some species that they need

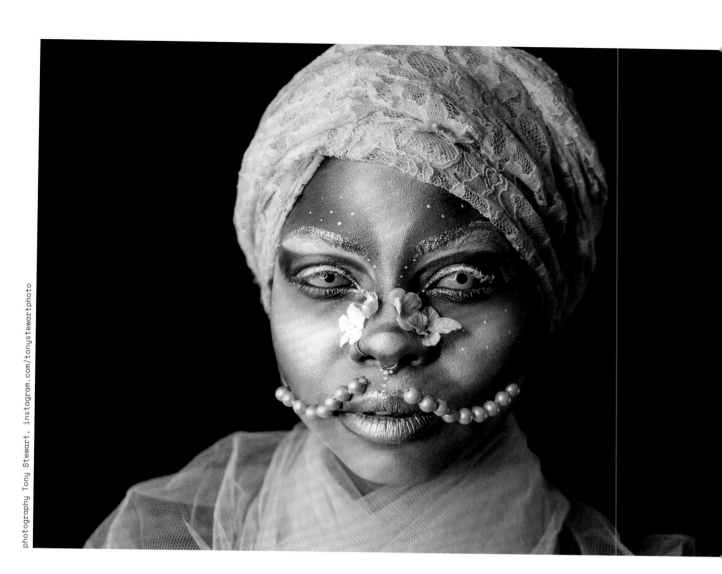

photography Tony Stewart, instagram.com/tonystewartphoto

photography Stephanie Ballantine, instagram.com/stephanieballantine

Every decision I make in a drawing or a piece feels loaded with meaning, and it can be quite personal when I am drawing in the stream of consciousness. I sometimes wonder why I do these things, why I give characters certain qualities. Why do all these characters have monobrows? Am I okay? But now my view is that it's not really important to ask yourself all these questions. Don't create obstacles for yourself, conceptually or otherwise, when letting work flow out of you; that's always going to be the most unique way of creating something. If you are finding it tough or unrewarding when it's personal work, it's only going to feel harder when making work for clients. You have to make sure it feels spontaneous and good.

Joseph Melhuish

Joseph Melhuish is
an animation direc-
tor and illustrator
based in London.
He is represented
by Strange Beast and
has created films for
Vice, MTV and Adult
Swim as well as ani-
mated illustrations
for Bloomberg and Red
Bull Music Academy.

josephmelhuish.com

Using Materials You Have No Idea How to Use

Brooklyn-based artist Jon Burgerman encourages mistakes, experiments and improvisation within his practice to allow for new, fun ways of making. His mission is to inspire creativity in others and to never know exactly what he will create next. His artworks are held in the collections of several institutions including the Victoria and Albert Museum, London.

jonburgerman.com

In 2014, I completed a project called *Small Edition*, a series of miniature sculptures after Jeff Koons, which resulted in a lot of left-over Play-Doh. I don't normally make sculpture, but I started creating these little Play-Doh characters. That's what I tend to do when I have a new material to play with, I try to make characters out of it. Then, at the beginning of the pandemic, when it hit New York, I would go for a walk every once in a while. The streets were very empty, which is unusual to see in Brooklyn; there's normally people everywhere. I started taking some photos and I thought, ah, I finally have somewhere to put these characters, I could deposit them into the photograph.

Jon Burgerman

I discovered that we have a box of watercolours at home, which I had never used before. I found all these scraps of paper, leftovers, and I started to make little blobs on them. It was exciting because it was something I had never done before, and it felt new. It was very meditative, very relaxing. It was a material I was unfamiliar with. I didn't really know what I was doing and didn't quite know how it works. I liked the fact that the colours bleed, that it was not too accurate. I just started making some blobs and as it's my way, began turning them into little characters, blob after blob after blob.

The more I made, the more I started reverting to type. I tried making them into characters, giving them more defined features, making them figurative. That was totally ok, but along the way it got more complex and I felt myself aiming towards something. Whereas the original joy came from not knowing what the hell I was doing.

Maria Filipe Castro
is a toy artist from
Portugal. With her
Droolwool project,
she tells tiny sto-
ries with a touch of
innocence and humour.
She plays with ste-
reotypical expres-
sions and makes her
deliciously cute
characters portray
spontaneous human
reactions: pure joy,
disappointment and
tenderness.

droolwool.com

Droolwool

Playing with Patterns

Jing Wei is a Chinese-born, Brooklyn-based illustrator. Her work ranges from graphic, conceptual images to large-scale murals and textured works on paper. Her visual stories often exhibit a surreal quality and use people and everyday situations as a backdrop for the unexpected.

jingweistudio.com

Jing Wei

My compositions tend to be very grounded in minimal action. I love working with a pattern-like foundation because I feel that repetition can be so visually impactful. I like to play around with that and play around with the relationships between my characters, seeing how this can change based on experimenting with the formation.

Hattie Stewart

The Colour Pink Should Be Celebrated!

Hattie Stewart is a self-proclaimed 'professional doodler' with a unique and playful illustration style that extends itself through the worlds of advertising, art and fashion. Her drawing over the covers of influential publications such as *Interview*, *Vogue*, *i:D* and *Playboy* has formed the basis for most of her commercial projects and endeavours. Her work is bold and experimental in application, enabling her to eschew the more traditional boundaries within the field of illustration.

hattiestewart.com

Pictoplasma: I would like to start at the beginning, to understand how you found your own voice; because you have a very strong visual identity and voice.

Hattie Stewart: Thank you, that's very nice to hear. I've drawn obsessively ever since I was a child. You never really know which direction your style is going in or what something is going to become until you're at a place where you have enough to look back on. Then you see; oh look, I was exploring that back then, and that it's all a journey. I was drawing cartoons and replicating what I saw in my comics; *Beano*, *Dandy*, *Beryl the Peril* or *Micky Mouse*. Inevitably, those influences embedded themselves in the core of my work. There's always going to be some kind of link and story there. It's very different today because as a child, I could barely hold a pen. Now, I think I'm more or less competent! But yeah, it's interesting to reflect on the journey.

P   As a child, you were probably more into cuteness than today. People would say hearts and flowers and all the colourful cheeky stuff you do is still very cute. But I would say that it's so cute it makes your eyes bleed. It's about the aggressiveness of cuteness. Can you relate to that?

H   Yeah, it's the same with being called kitsch; it can be a little bit offensive. I get labelled 'cute' a lot, and it's not a word I'm really a fan of. I think that being a woman and inevitably doing more feminine characters or shapes means that you just get put into that box. There's always a darker undertone to my work, and weirdly, when I was a child, I drew really horrible stuff. In uni I did a whole project called *Little Slices of Death*, which was gross. I did one vaguely pornographic graphic novel, which I shouldn't get into – it was vulgar. I have always had an underlying interest in the macabre. As a young illustrator trying to find some ground, there had to be some level of commercial activity in my work, and I think that's when the more playful characters came along. When people respond to those really positively, it's hard not to include them more in your work. But I always see the dark undertones.

P   Do you feel as though you're in a strong place in regards to being a woman? And do you feel that you are part of a new feminist movement?

There's always a darker undertone to my work.

ous and part satire; it's a collision of sorts between two ideas. It's a dislike of something, but it's also a love and obsession with something, whether that be beauty, or femininity or sex. I can never really answer a question with a very straight, clear answer, because it's always a conversation. One day I say I'm a feminist artist, the next day I say no, feminism has nothing to do with my work.

P   When did you start painting these magazine covers?

H   I was working in a bar in east London and was bored out my mind. I thought about what I could be doing and how to get my work out there. I was drawing away mindlessly over this picture of Lily Allen, then I just thought: Oh, that looks freaky, I kind of like that! And because I've always been an avid collector of magazines, I went home and got a huge pile and just started playing with it and drawing on them.

It was kind of gross, very punk graphic, not really what I do now, which I feel is more considered. It was something of an *attack*. But I recognised something interesting, something I really liked, and it was a nod to this stuff that I loved as a younger kid; a style that came out of the 1960s and 70s, like Martin Sharp with the Cream covers, *Disraeli Gears*, all my favourite stuff growing up and stuff that I studied in college. I came to an inevitable crossroads.

This work became pivotal in how I engaged with social media. When I shared this work, people really enjoyed it and I gained a following. That was obviously very encouraging. I carried on and on, and it slowly grew.

Now, in regards to commercial brands and stuff – which I hadn't originally

It was kind of gross, very punk graphic, not really what I do now.

H   This kind of conversation has gone on with female artists for years. I refused to use pink because it was considered feminine and therefore not important. Now it's like, well fuck it, if I want to use pink, I want to use pink. Why is that a negative thing? Why is something feminine seen as something negative? It should be celebrated. It's an incredibly strong and multi-toned colour. I love it. Even the art world is male dominated, so feminine themes make you feel that you could be excluded from certain areas. We're making our own areas now. Also, as an artist, I don't think that besides being a woman, I make feminist work. Other people may agree or disagree, but I don't necessarily like being called a female artist, or for my work to be described as being about my gender. Because it's not at all. My work is just my work. It's just stuff I like.

P   Let's take a look at the doodle bombing you do with erotic or porn magazine covers. You're a woman appropriating content that is targeted at male audiences, turning and twisting it into something different. I don't think you can take a gender-neutral perspective here, and that's good!

H   That's fair enough. In the context of the covers, they're part humor-

There's a very dismissive attitude that illustration is just an accompaniment to something else.

intended to get into – there's so many more demands on a project: it's not just advertising, what I produce is also going to be used as social media assets, stickers, product, in-store activation. There's a whole plethora. My work engaged with that very well. I was really fortunate that these opportunities arrived through exploring my work in my own way, how I wanted to express myself. I never wait for something to come to me. I just create what I want to make, and that brings in opportunities. It's all an exploration.

At one point, as with most artists, I felt the pressure of social media. If a big thing came out, like the infamous *Paper Magazine* cover 'Break

the Internet – Kim Kardashian', I felt that I had keep up with the momentum and constantly respond. Then I thought, that's not for me, that's for other people. That doesn't make me do good work. I realised that there was a long period where I was doing covers that were kind of gross. They weren't considered, and it was just so slapdash.

In the last couple of years, I've wanted to slow it down a bit, just focus on creating pieces that actually have a bit more context, that are more interactive and have more depth and detail. I don't feel that pressure to do things quickly because I need to get something online. Now it's rather, I'm going to create a piece of work

that I enjoy sitting with, that I'm visually excited by afterwards.

P The work is very two dimensional, really flat in a good sense, it's all about the surface. But you started doing exhibitions, bringing your work into three-dimensional space. Let's take a look at an exhibit you made in 2016.

H That was at *First Site Colchester*, which is actually in my hometown. They were doing an artist's room exhibition about Andy Warhol, and they'd seen my work and knew that I was a Colchester artist. They brought me on board to do my thing, and at that time I was really going in on the covers. They gave me a huge space. Considering I work so small, I wondered how I could make it engaging and interactive. One of the interesting things with the covers is 'the before and after'; the original context and how that context is transformed through illustration. I thought, how can I show that in a static space and make a 2D flat image come to life where you can see the flip between? Then I had the idea of making lenticular pieces, bringing the original and the illustrated sections together in one image.

We printed these lenticular images super, super big – A0 size – which was really cool. Then I decided to fly-poster, completely covering the entire room with all the magazine covers so it would be very intense and in your face. Because that's what media is like; we're constantly bombarded by it. The exhibition was a little nod to that.

P   As busy and radical as it was, it was still hanging pictures on the wall, even if you had two layers. But an exhibition you did later at Now Gallery, London, in 2018, was something else. You really played with the three-dimensionality of space and the two-dimensionality of your work.

H   I'm always thinking about how my illustration, which is flat on the page, can take up space and incorporate itself into space. I've made tapestries, lenticular prints, wallpaper boards… in every single show there's been an experiment and something a little different, a way for me to play. An exhibition space is often awkward or really big or really small with loads of corners. The Now Gallery is a huge, curved architectural space that's pretty much all glass with no walls. How on earth do I put my artwork into this space? For a few years, the idea of how I could make viewers physically part of the illustration had been on my mind,

I Don't Have Time For This, Now Gallery (2018)

and the mirrors installed in the space seemed to be a way to unlock that box. I've always wanted my work to have some kind of interactivity with the viewer because my work is in itself interactive with the covers, kind of like an inception. With this show, I thought: why don't I just take up the space with one big flat illustration? But it has layers within it, and then you lie down and look up, and you're a part of the illustration, of the art-work. It's a chaotic yet relaxing space. It's two halves. It was meant to be fun and have some level of engagement.

There's often a very dismissive attitude that illustration is just an accompaniment to something else, but it's so rich, there's so many forms of illustration, there's so many ways it can be applied and so many stories that are told. It covers so many incredible bases. Ever since I was in uni – an incredible but traditional university where I didn't always fit in – I've been thinking of ways in which I can demonstrate illustration in its full range of capabilities and thus elevate it as the incredible artform that it is. I used to dislike being called an illustrator; I wanted to be called an artist. But now, I'm like; No, I want to be an illustrator because we're doing pretty well!

P   I think that's an amazing plea and advocacy for the genre of illustration. I feel totally the same, but I feel that illustration has changed, and you are part of that change. Thank you so much.

Pop Magazine (2020)

Jim Stoten is an illustrator who works from his home in Hastings for clients all over the world. His sketch-books are elaborate compositions that channel his stream of consciousness, and his drawings have a psychedelic flair. Jim has just released his album *Lights* on pink vinyl through Dirty Melody Records, recorded on a 4-track tape recorder.

jim-stoten.com

Jim Stoten

This gatefold image of my album *Lights* started as a drawing
based on a photo of Paul McCartney with a small brass band
whilst recording *Sgt. Pepper's Lonely Hearts Club Band*, which
expanded from there as I tried to visualise the feeling that
I wanted to achieve with the music on my album.

● Over the past fifteen years, I've worked on hundreds of projects using different tools to generate visual and audio-visual pieces. I have always been trying to find matching points between poetry, design, technology, comedy, characters and education.

● I like to think of visual poetry as a place where we go to exercise and rehearse certain concepts and create symbols. Also, where we can find patterns and questions that help us express ourselves more genuinely.

● With design, I'm attracted to the construction of aesthetics and systems. I'm obsessed with the consistency of my aesthetic codes. I enjoy the idea of building a design system and applying its rules and seeing the results that are generated.

● I'm attracted to technology for its irreverence. I'm lured by its light and by its darkness. For example, because there are so many ways in which virtual reality can be used in an incorrect way, I feel a moral duty to look for the right one. Even if I don't use it to generate content on social media or to get a project, it seems to me that this genuine search to find a useful and correct way to use a technology must always exist. I have the same feeling about augmented reality and machine learning or any intelligent automation process. I believe it's my responsibility to find the right and optimal way for it to be used. With these technologies, the easiest thing is to exploit the user, or blame the end of the world on them. I believe that the most difficult and important thing concerning a new and powerful technology is to find its optimal utility to create symbols and concepts, without harming or taking advantage of people.

● Regarding comedy, I like to understand it as a construction of rhythm, timing and editing. It's extremely fascinating, this search to find a rhythm to be able to connect with the person in front of you.

● And if we talk about characters, I really like thinking about them as complex and powerful tools when it comes to defining concepts. That is, I don't use them because they are gentle, or because I like to draw them, or watch them move around the screen. It is rather because I am interested in characters as great bridges between something inside our heads with something that is outside.

● Finally, when it comes to education, I think it is essential to connect to other creatives and build a fresh community that asks itself a lot of questions and goes out and explores how to answer them. The struggle to build a better space for expression and education is always going to be collective.

Tomás García
co-founded animation
studio PepperMelon
in 2007 as creative
director, producing
character driven CGI
projects for a wide
range of clients. In
2015, he moved on to
focus more on his own
projects, conceptual
based workflows, aug-
mented and virtual
reality, character
development, images
and videos for a
variety of projects
including — but not
limited to — commer-
cials, music, apps,
games, posters,
magazines, installa-
tions and objects. In
2019, Tomás opened a
YouTube channel to
connect with new gen-
erations of creatives
in his region.

tomasgarcia.tv

Tomás García

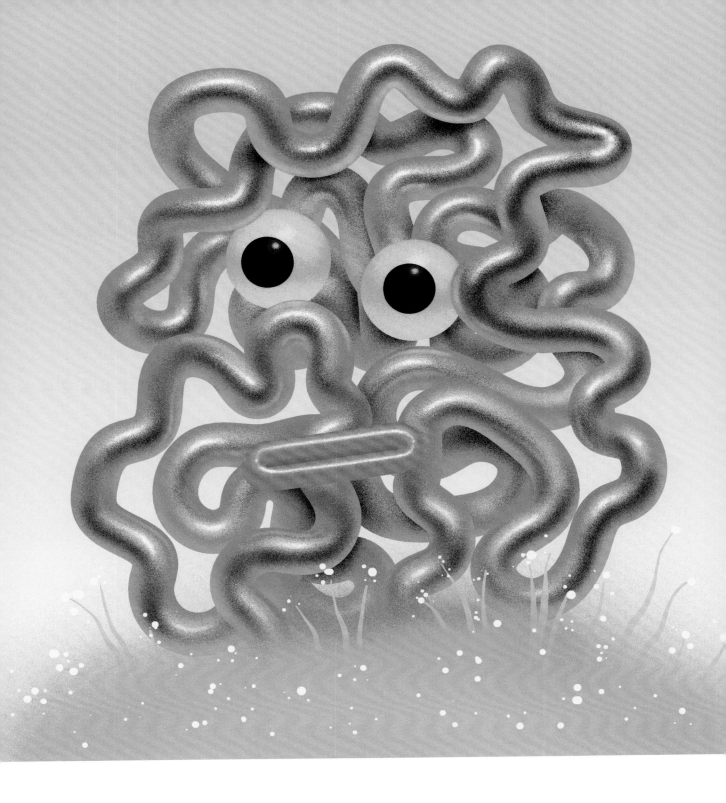

Alex Kiesling is a
Brooklyn based illus-
trator and animation
director. His work is
heavily inspired by
toys and the escapism
that our imagination
gave us as kids.
He brings colours,
shapes and textures
often associated
with childhood into
his contemporary
illustration and
animation, reminding
audiences that it's
okay to feel like
a kid again.

alexkiesling.com

Alex Kiesling

I always find myself imitating the characters I am making! Talking to them is a way of asking: How do they sound? What are they thinking? What are their emotions? It is similar to being a method actor, it makes me familiar with what I am making.

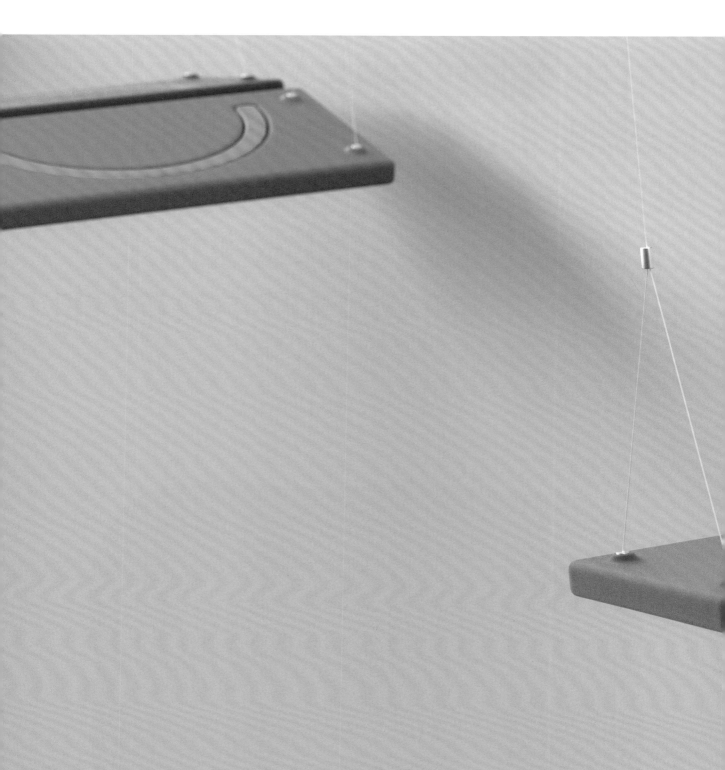

Italian-born
designer, animator,
and director Lucas
Zanotto's career is
as varied and play-
ful as his creations.
His work effortlessly
merges analogue and
digital craft into
thought-provok-
ing films, apps and
installations. Lucas
also creates intrigu-
ing apps for children
through his enter-
tainment platform
YATATOY, which aims
to encourage crea-
tivity through music
and art.

lucaszanotto.com

Lucas Zanotto

Maximizing Minimalism

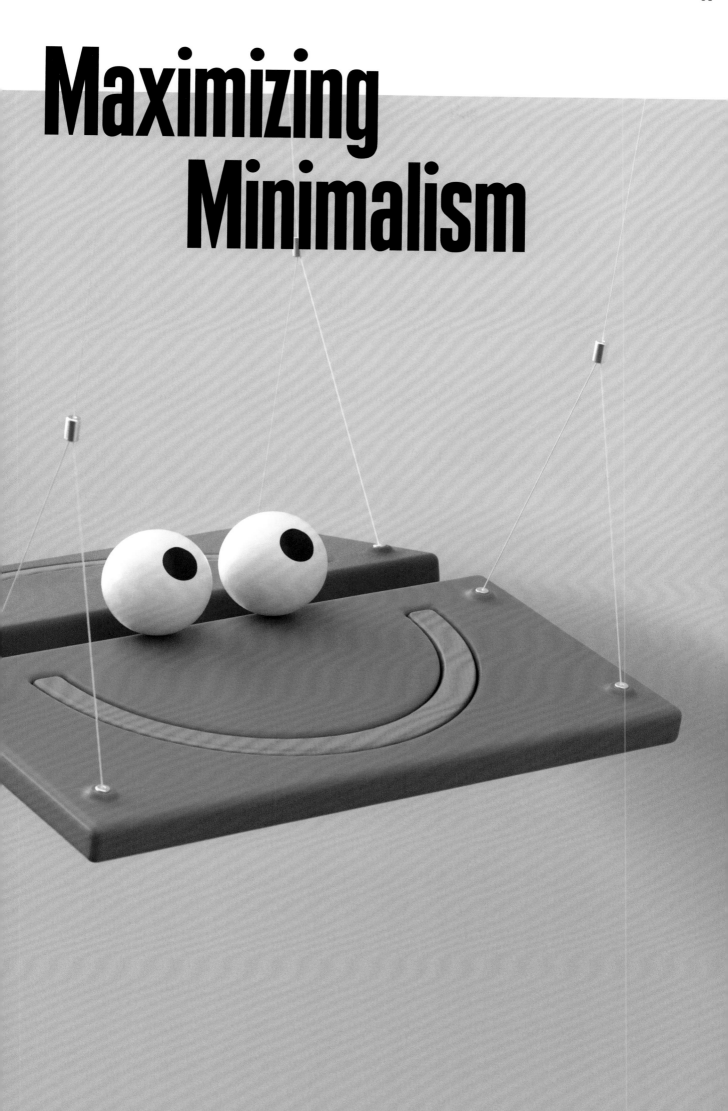

For years, I have been working as a director mixing different media and types of animation. This year, I started playing with 3D software, putting together simple shapes and adding eyes onto them. At first, I made a series of animals, then hands, then abstract shapes. I tried to capture a realistic feeling. Combining different shapes with simplistic forms to express an emotion worked really well. I continued making loops in which different moods change. People responded really positively, and I was heartened to get feedback from people with anxiety or panic attacks who wrote that they often go back to my account because it relaxes them.

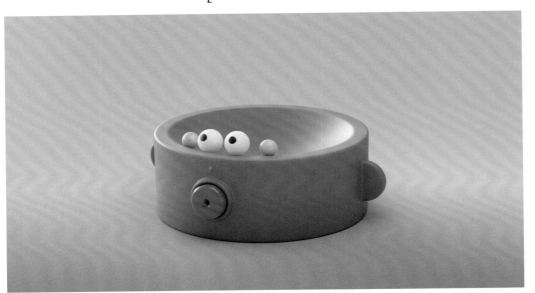

It's funny; I gathered a following, and by doing these side projects, I became 'the 3D guy' – but I am so not the 3D guy! I don't know a lot about 3D, I just try stuff out and keep learning. It's just a fun way to explore shapes. It has a similar feeling to building stuff by hand, which I really enjoy as well; it comes close to building something for real. It gives me a very similar sense of satisfaction.

If I look at all my work over the years, there is a consistent style. I think that's key because that is you. It's not that you decide to cultivate a certain style, but it comes with your personality, the things you like, the colours you like. You filter what you like and it becomes you. It evolves over time and you bring in other things but the things that you really like stay, and over time it's a sticky ball that rolls and keeps growing with the stuff you like.

Aman Khanna

Embracing Imperfection

Aman Khanna has turned his interest in clay into a full-time studio and gallery. With his team, he produces sculptures and objects that have been exhibited at the London Design Fair, in Istanbul, New York, Hong Kong and throughout India.

claymen.in

Pictoplasma: You studied graphic and information design in London almost 20 years ago and then set up your graphic design studios in London and New Delhi. A few years ago, you changed direction and started working with clay. Can you talk about how that shift took place?

Aman Khanna: In 2013, after working for more than a decade with digital media, I'd had enough of my world being confined to the screen and I wanted some tactility. I joined the Pictoplasma Academy in that year, which gave me the push I needed, and right after that I took another course to learn how to work with clay; this being the most ancient medium used by people to create everyday objects. I quickly turned off my mobile phone, I stopped taking calls from my clients, I was literally just immersed in clay and spent a couple of months working with it, learning how to hand-mould it. There has been no stopping ever since.

I started to create small clay sculptures that were inspired by my surroundings and the people living in them. These became the *Claymen*. They are divided into two broad categories; functional and dysfunctional. The functional pieces may or may not have faces, but the dysfunctional are mostly characters and depict different feelings and emotions. They are all based on human behaviour.

P   Working with clay means that all your pieces are individual, and you embrace the idea that there's beauty in little imperfections. Is this intrinsic to your progression from digital to analogue?

A   I think so. Once I got familiar with the material of clay, I realised that the more natural it remained, the better it looked. At least, to my mind. I had seen a lot of really clean, polished sculptures but I just wanted the form and finish to come out of the material itself, so I left it bare. A lot of the pieces I make are completely unglazed, and each piece retains its individuality.

P   Can you tell us more about this distinction between the functional and dysfunctional pieces?

A   The idea for the dysfunctional pieces was that things obviously don't run smoothly all the time and there are issues and discrepancies. They are inspired by observations about myself and other people and how they are interacting; what they are saying and what they are not saying. These objects were statements on what was going on. For instance, this one work, *Self-Reflection* (2017), is about trying to understand how I am responding to certain things. When people walk into the studio and see this work, they instantly have a connection to it because at some point they are also faced with a similar internal conversation. A lot of my pieces are like that, evoking conversations, and that is what makes people relate to them.

P   Would you say that this dysfunctionality is also a comment on society?

A   The moment you make something, it acquires a space. I was working digitally before, so everything stayed in files and folders. The moment I started sculpting, this changed and I keep asking myself; why am I even making something? For me, the answer is that it's all about making a statement, trying to say something psychological that people can relate to, understand about themselves or their interactions with other people. This resonates. People come into the studio to buy a functional piece, but they end up buying a dysfunctional sculpture.

Self-Reflection (2017)

Pictofolio is Pictoplasma's online home for characters – and their creators. The community website offers international artists, illustrators and designers a unique platform to share their art, inspire each other, research trends, meet new friends, collaborate and show character.

pictofolio.com

Postcards from

Alexis Tapia
Las Californias, Mexico
@elpingu

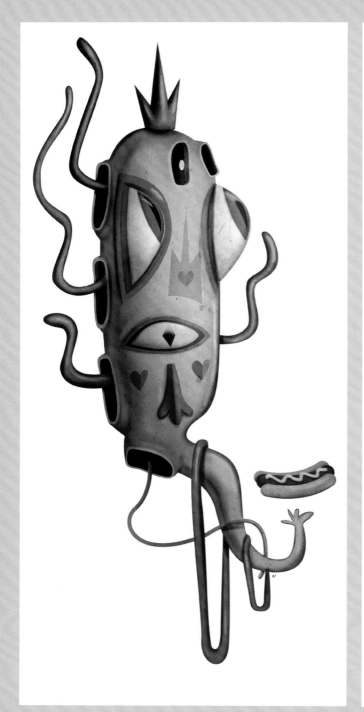

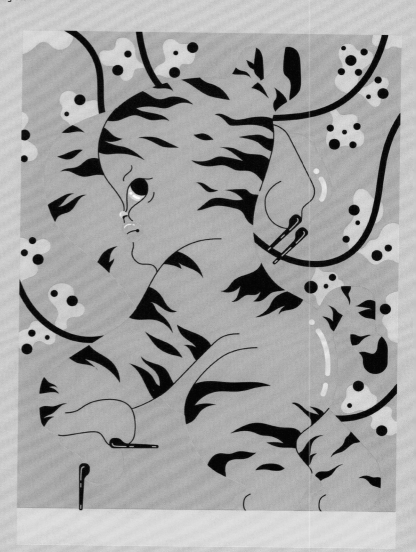

Karin Kraemer
Hamburg, Germany
@karin_kraemer

Luiza Kwiatkowska
Warsaw, Poland
@luikwiatkowska

Miguel Guercio
Caracas, Venezuela
@miguel_guercio

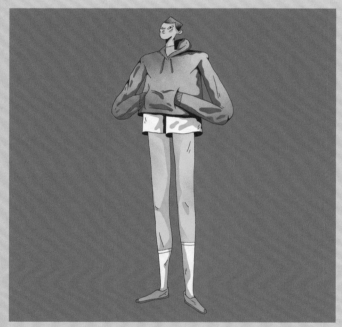

Peter Javidpour
Los Angeles, United States
@peterjavidpour

Sergio Casado
Madrid, Spain
@sergiocasado

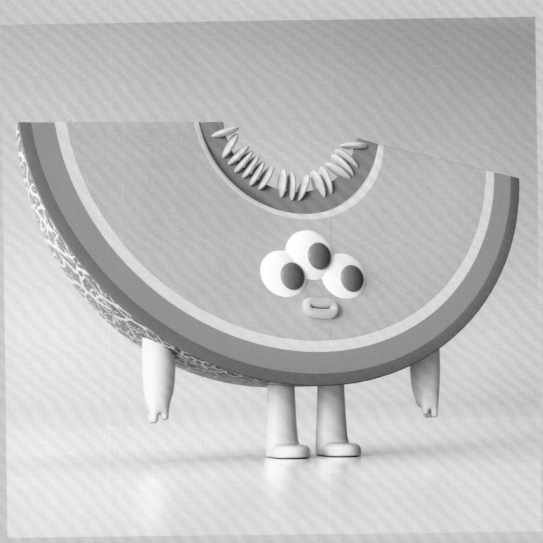

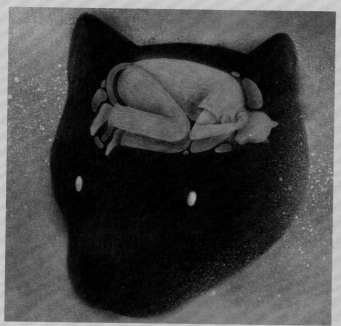

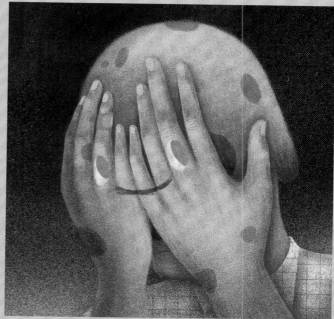

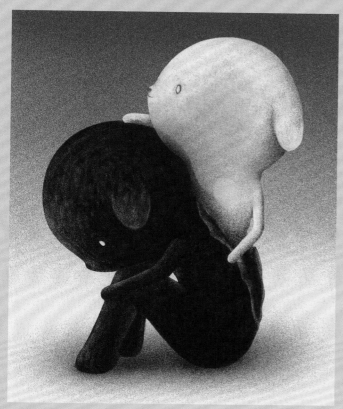

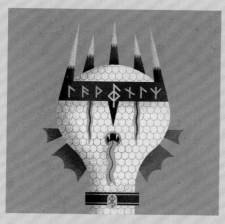

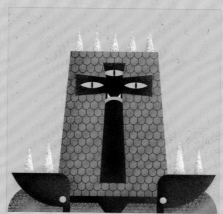

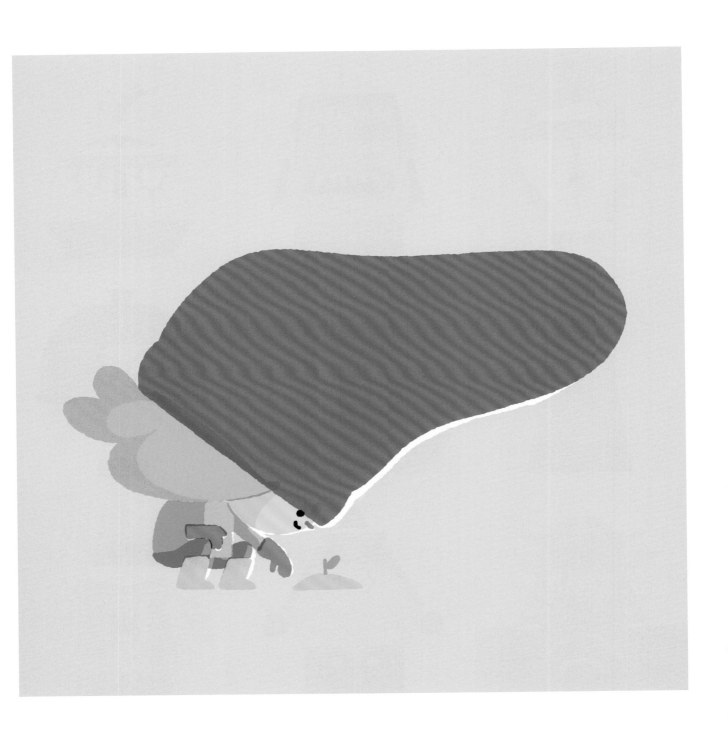

Thanks for the Tangerines

As everyone went into lockdown all over the world, it struck me how little my day to day life changed because I work at home. But I was still completely overwhelmed by everything that was happening. I couldn't concentrate and found myself checking the news constantly. It seemed to me that going to bed for however long the pandemic would last might actually be sensible.

I noticed that I was seeing all the changes in the neighbourhood the same way as you do when you travel somewhere. When you first arrive, everything feels new and incredibly interesting. People who were not normally at home or in their gardens were suddenly there, and one morning I saw a teeny-tiny girl in the tallest, reddish-orange beanie I had ever seen. She was in her garden with her family and captured my imagination. I went home and drew her right away.

I don't normally post my work on Instagram on a daily, or even weekly basis, simply because most of the projects I do take a long time and I need to wait for them to be released before I can show them off. But I posted this drawing instantly and decided that I should do a drawing every day of something I saw on my walk. Doing that would become part of my daily routine, something personal and low stakes, mainly to keep me distracted.

It was the beginning of spring, and the colours were intense and bright. I took photos of the flowers, and those colours were the inspiration for the colour palette in all these drawings. It's a time when the light is glowing, and early in the morning and in the evening, there are long shadows. The trees were full of citrus too, and I saw a basket filled with tangerines that was replenished every day. That also became part of my routine; picking up a tangerine and eating it on the way home.

Rilla Alexander
is a designer, illus-
trator and picture
book maker whose
work has appeared on
everything from toys
and tea cups to bus-
ses and buildings.
Her alter-ego Sozi
stars in her picture
books *Her Idea* and
*The Best Book in the
World*, and she has
illustrated stories
by Jane Yolen
and Lemony Snicket.

byrilla.com

Hel Covell is an
illustrator from
Yorkshire, UK, whose
work encompasses
bright and playful
characters. Her debut
picture book *Jumble
Wood* was published by
Nobrow / Flying Eye
Books (2018). When
staging exhibitions,
Hel likes to exper-
iment with various
media, from ceramics
to installation.

helcovell.com

I want my work to have a balance between colourful (but not cute) and sensual (but not sexual).

Marylou Faure is a
French illustrator
and artist, currently
based in London.
Marylou's career has
seen her working on
many personal pro-
jects and collabo-
rations with global
brands that focus on
social and ethical
issues, reflecting her
intention to tackle
the issues she cares
about,

maryloufaure.com

Marylou Faure

Guillaume Kashima –
also known as FFwG –
is a French illustra-
tor living in Berlin.
His background as a
graphic designer in
advertising formed
his direct and mini-
mal approach to image
production. While
Guillaume's aesthet-
ics are versatile,
his process always
originates from bold-
ness, wit and humour.

guillaumekashima.com

Guillaume Kashima

Exploring Uncertain Grounds

Paolo Puck is a British-born artist currently residing in the United States. Originally trained as an illustrator, he now works primarily in sculpture; a field in which he is self-taught. Best known for his bizarre, whimsical and dreamlike creations rendered in needle-felted wool, Puck's sculptures give viewers a glimpse of a world inspired by myths and fairytales, Jungian theory and Gnosticism. Puck has exhibited in the United States and abroad, with exhibitions at Nucleus Portland, Portland, OR; Samek Art Museum, Lewisburg, PA; Jonathan Levine Gallery, NY, NY and the Royal Scottish Academy, Edinburgh, Scotland, UK.

paolopuck.com

Pictoplasma: The references you draw on for your characters come from far and wide, including early civilisation, Ancient Greek, Roman and Medieval artworks and Japanese theatre. How do you balance working with these references and developing your own aesthetics?

Paolo Puck: I find that a subject will fascinate me for a while, for example, medieval pilgrim badges, and I'll spend ages researching and looking at them. Eventually, I kind of lose interest and find something else. It's often not until later that I'll look back at my work and say, 'oh, it definitely had a flavour of that!', but it's rarely direct or intentional.

I suppose it's like hanging out with someone for a while; you take on aspects of their personality. Even though you still have your own way of being, there are now a few other shades thrown in there too. The influence is initially strong, and eventually only an echo remains, but it still shapes you.

P How do you approach making a work? What's the relevance of concept, sketching and design to the actual making or sculpting?

PP I actually do a shockingly small amount of prep work. A quick sketch or plasticine model is about as much as I do. The rougher the sketch, the better.

I don't like to be completely bound to those original concepts and designs. I like for pieces to be themselves and find their own way into being.

I often just zone out when sculpting and get lost in the flow of the forms, paying no attention to the big picture. Pouring my energy into a new piece through sculpting like that feels like the best way to tap into a pure creative process and bring something into the world that has its own spirit.

P A mask is a medium of transformation: visually, to change appearance, socially, as a way to transform the position of the person wearing it in a ritual and for the self, it is a confrontation with our inherent otherness and dimensions of reality. What is your interest in masks?

PP I'm not sure why masks are something I'm drawn to. I tend to just make things that I feel compelled towards without trying to overthink why, but sometimes I reflect on those things later on. For example, the witch character was something that I continuously came back to in my work. If you had asked me at the time, 'what's with the witch theme?' I'd probably have said, 'I think witches are neat'. But on reflection, it's about a troubled childhood with an alcoholic and mentally unwell mother.

A lot of my themes revolve around the blurred lines between something that's safe or dangerous and beautiful or ugly. On one hand, my mother was meant to be my carer but on the other, she was often a threatening figure that I couldn't feel safe around. I often explore things in my work that are supposed to be safe and comforting but can instantly flip into the antithesis of those things. Being on that uncertain ground is a common thread in my work.

I have an early memory from childhood of a scary old woman who lived on our street. I suppose we thought she was a witch of sorts and we were told to keep away from her. When my mother was having an episode of alcohol-fuelled psychosis, I would convince myself that the scary old woman had climbed inside my mother's skin, and it was the old woman who was controlling her and making her act so menacing and strange. I suppose these ways of understanding the human psyche through a mask have been with me from very early on.

P Are you interested in the performative aspect of masks?

PP Most definitely. My first experience with mask making was for Samhain performances (the Gaelic festival marking the end of the harvest season and beginning of winter), which I took part in when I lived in

Self Portrait with Pompoms (2016)

Scotland. One of the reasons I haven't made many masks in the last couple of years is because it feels like such a dead experience to just trot out these costumes for a photoshoot, besides having the thrill of scaring the odd dog walker in the process! I'd love to get back to making characters that are brought to life with performance, but I haven't found a crowd for that here in the US.

P   Your characters often have their mouths partly open, showing teeth, biting their tongues. How did this expression come about? Is there any inspiration for that, any reference, a feeling or attitude that motivates you?

PP   This is another thing that only became significant to me upon deeper reflection. As with my interest in masks, I think that the mouth obsession also partly comes from childhood.

I was never really taken to the dentist as a child and never taught how to brush my teeth or take care of my mouth. This neglect and years of not seeing a dentist meant that my mouth became a serious source of not only severe pain but also anxiety and shame, from late childhood onwards.

It's not something I consciously think about much, but mouths are definitely an important feature in my work. Those things that we push to the back

of our minds leak out the most through the art that we make.

P   You recently shifted your attention away from masks and costumes to sculptures. What can we expect in the future?

PP   As an artist, I'm not sure I'll ever settle on doing one thing only. I'm trying to become more at ease with letting chapters come to a close. Then I can take what I've learnt from them and move forward. I'm trying not to pay too much mind to what others might expect from me.

At the moment I'm working on a range of weird and, to be honest, horrendously ugly furniture. It's been nice to work

on some quicker and totally carefree projects, with no expectations for their success. I felt as though I needed to loosen up with my work and explore some ways of making that might suit me better.

The success of past projects can sometimes be a burden. It can hinder creative freedom, and I was really starting to feel that. I was starting to become worried about taking chances and making bad work, and if you're not careful that can stunt you as an artist. I'm taking some time to shed that and make some completely mad things!

The Visitors from Sirius B (2016), photo by K. Scott Kreider

Cabeza Patata is
an illustration and
animation studio in
Barcelona, created
by Katie Menzies
and Abel Reverter
in 2018. They care
about diversity and
female empowerment
and create a world
of playful yet strong
characters, full
of energy and posi-
tivity.

cabezapatata.com

Cabeza Patata

Our characters all have more or less the same proportions, which is probably why you often can't tell if you are looking at a woman or a man. When we show our work, people often ask,

'Which one's the woman?'

But does it really matter? We like to explore the possibilities of exaggerating characters without pushing stereotypes.

Where Is Dan?

I like to bring a certain level of detail into my illustration work, in both idea and execution. I like to think everything through. When I approach a crowd scene, the first thing I have to consider is how to convey the most important information. I lay out where I will place key elements, then I work through my gags and try to find a position for them. The idea is to create a scene that draws your eye in and allows you to breathe and explore at your own pace, rather than revealing the message right away. I want to keep you in my little 'Dan Woodger world' to explore. Thinking through my world like this is helpful. I like to know what's beyond the frame. And I like to put myself in it; I literally draw myself into every crowd scene as a character.

Having spent most of his childhood watching *The Simpsons*, it is perhaps no coincidence that illustrator and animation director Dan Woodger's colourful and cartoonish characters are bright-eyed and emotive, exuding a classic-retro feel and always with an undercurrent of wit about them. Dan is represented in the US and UK by Jelly.

danwoodger.com

Will Anderson is a
BAFTA winning writer
and director from the
Scottish Highlands.
He is currently
developing a feature
project *A Cat Called
Dom* and the game
Plaything.

wanderson.co.uk

Will Anderson

Laurie Rowan

The Joy of Quirky 3D

Every project starts with drawing; a lot of stream of consciousness drawing, with no preconceived notion about what I
am going to do. I just hope that I encounter something that
interests me. When I model, I like to stick to this original,
instinctive drawing style. The temptation is always there
to clean up but I need to fight that as much as I can. Instead
of correcting, I redraw until I find that satisfying mixture
of quirks that make up the composition.

I have sketchbooks full of impassive, dead faces. I don't like
my characters to be defined by a single emotional response.
Instead of feeling that my characters are my creations, I prefer
to feel as though I have simply encountered them and saved
a bit of the audience's reaction for myself as an observer.
I generally don't model my faces but animate them by hand,
then apply them to the 3D mesh. This is because 3D can easily
become a cold aesthetic, and doing it my way feels more tactile
and human.

Laurie Rowan is an
animator, illustrato
and director based
on the South Coast
of England. After
a decade of working
within the creative
industries for chil-
dren's animation and
high-profile clients,
he branched out with
his personal work,
which has been met
with global acclaim.
Laurie is represente
by Nexus Studios.

laurierowan.com

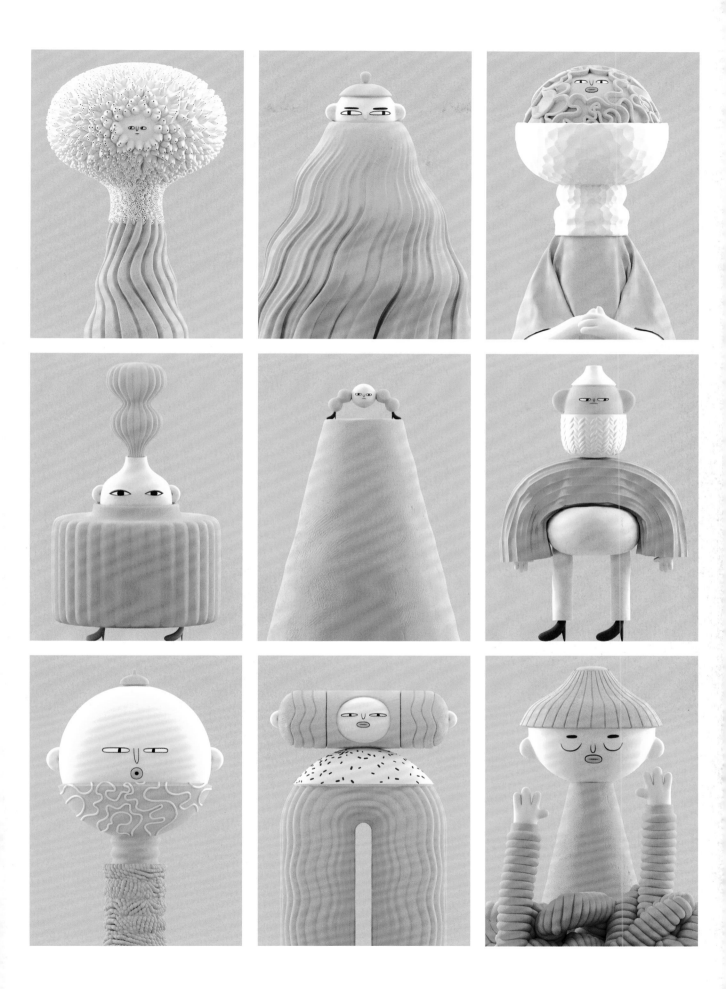

Haein Kim

My ethos is to make design that's fun, fresh and funny. I try to interpret all my characters and subject matter as women of colour because it's something that's important to me. I really want to contribute in giving people like me a platform to be seen, represented and celebrated.

Haein Kim is an illustrator, 2D animator and director based in Sydney. After graduating with her much acclaimed film *Peepin* (2018), in collaboration with her partner Paul Rhodes and based on her childhood experiences as a young Korean growing up in majority white Australia, Haein currently shares a studio with four other creatives next to a bangin' pub in the city.

haein-kim.net

Nadine Kolodziey

Nadine Kolodziey
is a visual artist
based in Frankfurt
and Berlin. During
her creative resi-
dency with Adobe,
she combined materi-
als such as plastic
and pixels to create
work that was hand-
cut, melted or trans-
formed into walkable
augmented reality
environments.

nadinekolodziey.com

Losing Public Space and Natural Connection

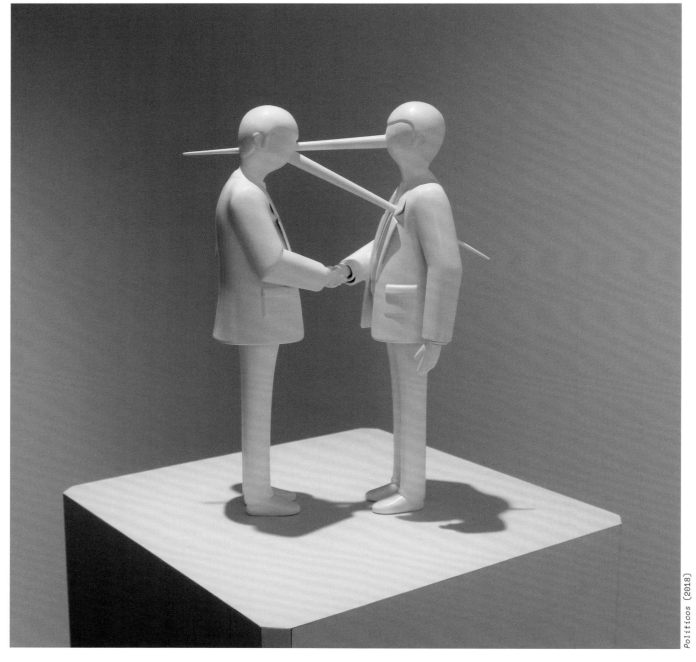

Pictoplasma: Is there something you can identify as a common thread running through your work, by way of introduction?

Doma: The work of Doma has a social commitment and is inspired by what is going on in the world; the reality, especially the worst things of reality, the things that are not really nice. And we try to do something with it.

P   When you began twenty years ago, you quickly found your way of bringing graphical images to the street. How did that happen?

D   We studied at the public university in Buenos Aires where we had a lot of information but no tools. When you study at a public university, you have to be able to do many things yourself, nobody will do much for you. We started to do things and bring them to the streets and public places. The public space in 2001 in Argentina was in total anarchy. It was the best place ever for young people because you could do whatever you wanted. I have the best memories of that time. No police, no state, no government, nobody – so we spent the whole day on the street. We could really do what we wanted. No money, no job; the only thing we could do was join friends and do things together. We got the public space because of the crisis. The doors were open. Even the police came to us and said, 'cool, guys', because they couldn't do much with us. At that time, all the art galleries and institutions were totally different from today, really structured and old-school. Public space was the place to be at that moment and it's probably the same again now because we are losing that space again.

P   Let us turn to your latest project, the exhibition *Naturaleza Muerta* at Centro Cultural Recoleta in Buenos Aires in 2018.

D   The exhibition is a trip through life, but starting from death. We believe we are kind of dead at the moment. You enter the exhibition through an installation of coffins and throughout the exhibition you cleanse yourself of guilt and are reborn at the end. We were trying to push people to question if they want to be part of this life; the life they saw in the exhibition.

The idea and all the artworks for this exhibition are part of a reaction and catharsis. We started seeing how our environment, how our friends and families, started to change with the screens and all the platforms that are proposed to us. Today, we are losing the natural connection between people, we communicate everything through technology. We think that's sad.

One work, *Políticos*, started with a hand-drawn sketch that was more like a cartoon-style character. But for the final piece, we wanted something more realistic, more human-like. We tried things out but didn't like them. Finally, we mixed the first cartoon character with human proportions, and that was satisfying to us, as we kept the essence of the first drawing. The piece represents what politics is today. We can't find one politician in the world that we like, but they are taking care of this crazy situation. We are not in good hands.

Bienvenido (2018)

Doma is an artist
collective formed
in 1998 in Buenos
Aires, currently run
by Orilo Blandini
and Julian Manzelli.
With their origins
in urban art, they
have always situated
collaborative work,
experimentation and
DIY at the axis of
their practice. Doma
have exhibited their
work around the
world in cities such
as Berlin, Cologne,
Los Angeles, Moscow,
Santiago de Chile,
São Paulo and Buenos
Aires.

doma.tv

La Fuente de la Vida, photo by Martina Mordau (2018)

Big, Bold and Angry

What makes you different from others is not your style, that can change. I think it has to change over time, as no one can be the same person they were three years ago. Somebody once described my work as big, bold, unapologetic and also a bit angry. This is how I feel most of the time. So, don't be afraid to put yourself into your work! Even if no one else can understand it, it's part of who you are!

Genie Espinosa was head of marketing at an automotive company, but quit at the age of twenty-eight to become a freelance illustrator. Seven years later, having illustrated many children books, she faced what she recalls as her biggest burnout. Three years later, she is now more at ease with herself, working as an illustrator and exploring new media and genres that she feels attracted to.

genie-espinosa.
squarespace.com

Genie Espinosa

Resting Bitch Face

Ever since I was a small child, I haven't liked smiling much, and I still don't like to smile today. I guess the term we now have for this is 'resting bitch face', which I definitely have. It causes some misunderstanding, as people think I am mad when I am not. My face is not really the indicator of how I am feeling. That manifests itself in my work.

Miranda Tacchia

I started drawing on Post-its. Sketchbooks are uncomfortable
for me. It's too much pressure to have a book full of blank
pages. I feel pressure to do something impressive on every
page. With the Post-its, I found myself feeling less hindered,
my creativity less hindered. I felt more at ease. I would go
straight to ink, but if I screwed up I would just put another
Post-it on top of it. I started drawing on regular paper, but
if I messed up certain parts, I would still stick Post-its over it
and keep drawing.

As I did more of these drawings, I started writing captions.
I would draw the image first, then come up with a short story
that was just one sentence long and make that part of the piece.
A lot of the pieces deal with personal relationships and sexual
themes.

Miranda Tacchia works
as a character and
background designer
in the animation
industry in Los Ange-
les. Her personal
work has been featured
in galleries in Los
Angeles, San Fran-
cisco, Portland and
New York, as well as
magazines such as
Juxtapoz and *Printed
Pages*. Her book
Unimpressed will be
published by Fanta-
graphics later in
2021.

instagram.com/mrmtacchia

After completing her illustration studies in the USA, Cristina Daura moved back to Barcelona and spent several years hitting her head against a wall, crying, accepting horrible commissions and hating everyone. Things changed on the day she decided to concentrate solely on what she really liked: illustrating and drawing comics — her own way.

cristinadaura.tumblr.com

Cristina Daura

Animation can be your best friend

Sarina Nihei is a Japanese animation director and illustrator. Her graduation film from the Royal College of Art, *Small People with Hats* (2014), won several prizes at festivals around the world including OIAF, HAFF and British Animation Awards. Specialising in hand-drawn animation, she makes surreal short films and music videos.

cargocollective.com/ sarinanihei

Sarina Nih

Pictoplasma: Can you tell us how you got into animation?

Sarina Nihei: As a kid I was a bit fucked up. I used to do lots of afterschool activities, such as piano, classical ballet, violin and gymnastics, which were basically my duties back then. I hated them, but I loved drawing. And at some point, I realised that art was something I wanted to pursue. So, I went to Tama Art University in Tokyo, where I studied graphic design. In the second year we had the animation class, which was mandatory, and we were encouraged to do hand-drawn animation without any technical skills. As soon as I started, I was instantly hooked. One of my biggest influences back then was Priit Pärn's work, a legendary Estonian animation director. His animations and stories were beautifully constructed. I was just obsessed with his work when I was in uni. I decided to continue my education at the Royal College of Art in London, where I kept making a bunch of films using the same technique; hand-drawn on paper.

I made a film called *Small People with Hats* (2014) for my graduation project, which is a film about small people with hats who get killed in absurd circumstances. A main theme in the film was the feeling of despair and absurdity, because these feelings are always there. People die and you cannot get away

I am always interested in religions even though I am an atheist.

from death. But at the same time, I didn't want to make a film that was just dark and slow and boring, so I tried to make it as entertaining as possible.

P   That film certainly made some waves. What happened after that? Where did it lead you?

S   After graduating from the RCA, it took me a while to get commissions back in Tokyo. I went to a couple of job interviews in the beginning, but I got rejected by everyone. I guess I had no idea how to sell myself and my animation style. All I wanted was to keep doing my own films, so I started to work at a beer bar in Tokyo, which was fun. Luckily, I was invited to film festivals because of my graduation film. I was traveling to the festivals whilst working at the beer bar. And gradually, I started to get commissions, including illustration jobs for music videos. Making music videos is so fun, I always enjoy doing it and I've been fortunate to have worked with artists who generously let me do whatever I wanted.

P   The next film you did was *Rabbit's Blood* (2017).

S   It's a story about a society where there is a conflict between people who wear black clothes and those who wear red clothes, and there are rabbits living underground. I had this idea for a while before I got commissioned by *Random Acts*, which is a television show made by the British TV station, Channel 4. I always start by writing lots of words, and drawing at the same time. This

I guess I had no idea how to sell myself and my animation style.

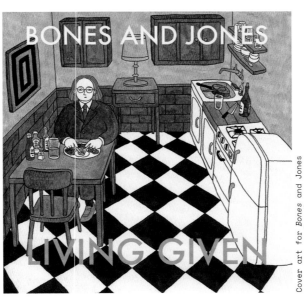

Cover art for *Bones and Jones*
Living Given (2017)

looks messy, but everything helps to build the world. This process is very important to me.

I got mentally and physically ill after making this film. I stopped thinking about new film ideas for a while. Gradually, I recovered, and when I was at a film festival in the Czech Republic, I was recommended to apply for an artist in residency program called Nippon Nordic, and I got in.

P   That's where you developed your latest film, which recently premiered in Ottawa, *Polka-Dot Boy* (2020).

S   It is a story about a boy who has polka-dot disease on his arms and is suffering from it, mentally and physically. One of the main subjects of this film was uncertainty surrounding the belief system of a cult or a religious group, because I am always interested in religions even though I am an atheist. I think there are a lot of things we can learn from religions, including the nature of belief. Again, I started with writing down a lot of words and drawing at the same time.

My films are always related to psychological things and unconsciousness and conspiracies because absurd things happen on a daily basis, and you can't predict what will happen next. Also, people die and you despair. Basically, it's a film about those things.

P   You have a very peculiar style and keep loyal to hand-drawn animation. Isn't it just too much work? And doesn't it feel outdated in these digital times?

S   People often ask me why I do hand-drawn animation because they think it's such a time-consuming thing to do, and it's true. It seems like the opposite of the animation trend that is digital, clean and beautifully designed. But I love how hand-drawn looks when it's finished, and drawing through tons of paper is quite therapeutic. Sometimes it's tough, of course. It feels like it takes forever, but most of the time, it's kind of fun. I find it so satisfying to look at the tons of paper when I'm done.

P   What do you do with these piles of paper? Do you keep them?

S   I've been keeping them since graduating from the RCA, and all my piles of papers are in my studio. I don't know what to do with them.

P   So, you are surrounded by them? You see them every day in their boxes?

S   Yeah, exactly. I think I'm gonna sell them in the future.

P   You said it gives you satisfaction, whenever you draw, to see all the work you have done growing into a bigger and bigger pile. I know this feeling of satisfaction. When something is finished, you can experience it over and over again. I wonder if this is a different kind of satisfaction to the feeling you have when you see the finished film?

S   The drawings that constitute my animation give me a certain satisfaction just after finishing the film because I don't know how people will react watching the film. In general, making animation is such a lonely process. Animation made me who I am, and I guess I enjoy every aspect of it. I've been fortunate to be able to do everything by myself. If you are single and lonely, animation can be your best friend.

Animation made me who I am.

Rabbit's Blood (2017)

Drawing, Dreaming, Changing

Three years ago, I quit my job in advertising, and my wife left me the same week. That broke me. I turned to sketching as a way of pulling my feelings out of myself. At the beginning, it was about dealing with chaos and not judging myself anymore. Every day, I would go to a coffeeshop and sketch for one hour. It didn't need to make sense. I just wanted to be out, sketching, as a way of channelling myself to do things that I'd always wanted to do but never had time for. That's how it started.

One day these characters arrived. Every character was bringing out my emotions in a way that I hadn't yet been able to do. I was developing a new kind of language – in my way, my voice – to speak out my feelings, my memories, the world around me. Inside there was an ocean, and the outside world was a shore; we keep crashing on to this shore, but we are changing all the time. That's what I learned: I was changing, we are always changing, and I was at peace with that.

I begin by sitting down and trying to relax. I often have my eyes closed, and I just sit there and write down the initial words that come into my head. From there, it is like looking at clouds. I start to see and shape things, and I arrive at a more conscious level. I start taking decisions, and I try to capture a situation in one frame – a feeling, a mood – with graphite. This gives them a raw quality, which I like a lot, and I try to see them in space; how they catch light and shadows. My English is terrible, and I often hear surreal things, surreal combinations of words. I try to take advantage of that, I harvest that, and I look into the weaknesses I have and try to have fun with it, be creative. It's silly, but I don't judge it, it's very fertile ground for me. I allow the part of me that doesn't understand things to just *play*. What matters is to play and not be too judgemental.

The world is weird, but the world has always been weird, and it always will be. There is no 'new normal'. We are changing, everything changes. My art taught me that I didn't want to go back to times when I was sad and depressed but to move forward and turn sadness into something good, bright, colourful and see the poetry in there. The world around us has no meaning until we look at it, hear it, feel it and put something out. It's nonsense to give feelings and thoughts to things that don't ask for it, but we keep doing it. As dark as it seems now, things will keep moving forward. We keep dreaming; we can dream better things and see the colour in things, see the bright side.

Trust your heart, that's the only thing that can give you direction. No one else can do it for you.

UntitledArmy are the broken pieces of the Brazilian artist, Lucas Camargo. Based in Brooklyn, he haunts coffee shops with his sketchbook, cursed by having to obsessively draw the stream of life and whatever comes to his mind. As a way to sustain this circus, Lucas directs 3D animations.

untitledarmy.com

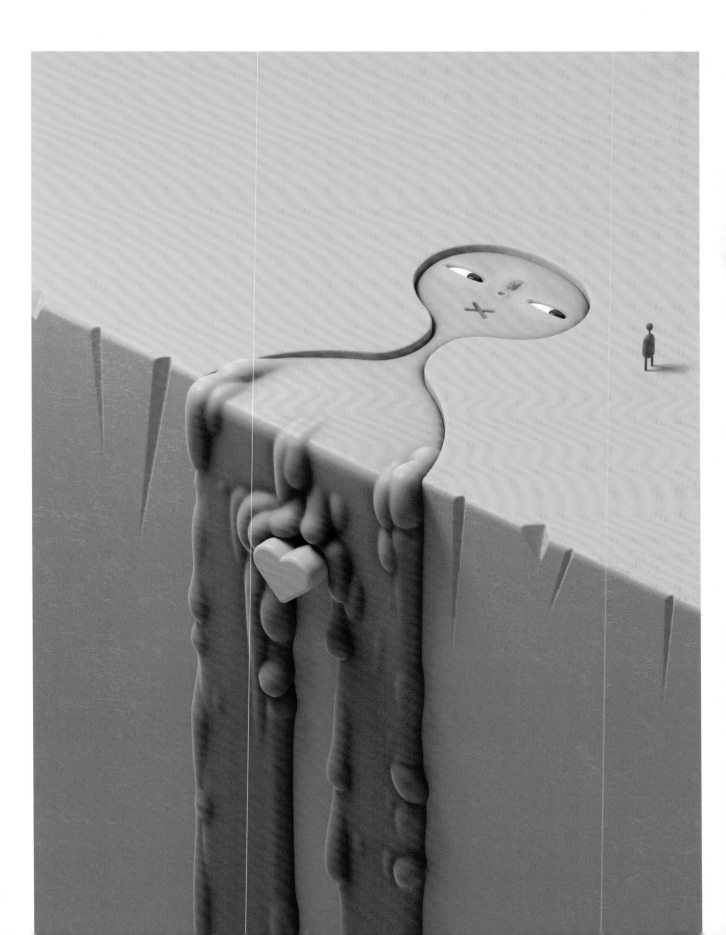

Pictoplasma Magazine
#1 FaceValue
Spring 2021

Publishers
Lars Denicke
Peter Thaler

Editorial Team
Anna Henckel-Donnersmarck
Nai Fowler
Sarah Schlüssel
Sophie Jackson

Copy Editing
Phoebe Blatton
phoebeblatton.blogspot.com

Cover
Melissa Carnemolla
pictofolio.com/artist/melissa_
carnemolla_

Art Direction & Graphic Design
Alexander Fuchs
Fides Sigeneger
fimasi.de

Print
Conrad
druckereiconrad.org

Typefaces
Plak
Lapture
Space Mono

Paper
LuxoArt Silk 250g
LuxoArt Silk 115g

Distribution
France
Interart
commercial@interart.fr

UK
John Rule Art Book Distribution
johnrule@johnrule.co.uk

All other territories
Pictoplasma
distribution@pictoplasma.com

This magazine has been published on the occasion of the 16th Pictoplasma Conference: Pictoplasma ~~2020~~ in Isolation, which took place as a free online broadcast on September 18th & 19th. Many of the interviews and artists' statements in this magazine are part of the artists' contributions and continue to be online on conference.pictoplasma.com/pictotalks

Funded by

HAUPT
STADT
KULTUR
FONDS

medienboard
BerlinBrandenburg

Pictoplasma
Plantagenstr. 31
13347 Berlin
Germany
pictoplasma.com | pictofolio.com

ISBN 978-3-942245-08-1